COMMON
SENSE
2.0

R. DAVID BRANDT

COMMON SENSE 2.0

A REVOLUTION TO ESTABLISH
REAL EQUALITY AND RESTORE
AMERICA'S MIDDLE CLASS

Common Sense 2.0
A Revolution to Establish Real Equality and Restore America's Middle Class

For information about this title or to order other books and/or electronic media, contact the publisher:

David Brandt Publishing
www.commonsense2book.com
rdbpublishing@gmail.com

ISBNs:
978-1-7355164-0-0 (hardcover)
978-1-7355164-2-4 (softcover)
978-1-7355164-1-7 (eBook)

Printed in the United States of America

Cover and Interior design: 1106 Design

This is dedicated to the great American historian
Clay Jenkinson, whose words inspired me to write this book.
Also, my eternal gratitude to my family, my wife, Ashlyn,
and children, Hallsey and Lucas, whose encouragement
sustained me through the process.

CONTENTS

PREFACE

I BEGAN WRITING THIS BOOK long before the murder of George Floyd in Minneapolis in May 2020. I had been tentatively working on it for about a year, and I honestly wasn't sure when the right time might be to publish a book like this. I can now see God's providential hand in the timing. While most every African American—and some portion of white America—have long been aware of police brutality, something about this event has finally captured the nation's attention.

Protesters in every state and throughout the world are now calling on the United States to live up to its own ideals, to provide the rights guaranteed by the Constitution to *every* American. It's going to be one hell of a fight, because no sooner did protesters hit the streets decrying police brutality than police came out with tear gas, flash bangs, clubs, and rubber bullets to prove them right. The fact that peaceful protesters were attacked for no reason shows that police departments will not easily accept reform.

I say all this because I don't think it's possible—or responsible—to write a book like this without acknowledging what appears to be a tipping point in our nation's history, a moment when we might finally come to terms with the consequences of slavery, America's original sin. People who are not of color cannot possibly understand what it's like to grow up black or brown in America. Yet, many of them *are* beginning to understand what it's like to have their lives controlled by powerful interests, to have their incomes slashed, to live without affordable healthcare, to see the wealthy and powerful gorge themselves on corporate welfare while others suffer.

Please forgive what might be an awkward transition, but quite possibly, these marginalized Americans are beginning to recognize what it's like to be used and manipulated by powers beyond their control. If so, a coalition might emerge, a coalition of peaceful revolutionaries, forming a movement to take back their country.

Some have not yet awoken. If you're one of them, I write this book for you. It's okay. It's not normal to jump into politics, at least not the way politics is currently being practiced. It's not normal to crave political power for its own sake. No matter—*you* can help us become the America that we were supposed to be. There's still time, but not a lot.

Right now, our nation is going through a phase that, in one way, mimics previous patterns, but in another, is something altogether new. By every metric that matters, 90 percent of our country is losing ground. Our quality of life is eroding while the one percent are doing better than ever. Forgive the cliché, but the American dream has become a nightmare. Time to wake up.

★

INTRODUCTION

L ET'S BEGIN WITH A QUICK-AND-CONCISE REVIEW of humankind's time on Earth, focusing specifically on how we have helped and harmed one another. It won't take long, because, as much as we've progressed in areas of technology, medicine, and creature comforts, human nature has not changed all that much through the millennia. In the beginning, we were just a small group of sparsely scattered people. As our population grew, we began to congregate and started working together, sharing our collective knowledge. Okay, I can already sense your boredom, but stay with me. It will make sense.

As we advanced, some became ambitious. They got people to work for them, building vast enterprises which elevated their own standard of living—which makes perfect sense and still does. However, others decided they wanted more, and the easiest way to accomplish this was to pay their workers less. In the absence of a democratic form of government, things quickly spun out of control. There were societies composed of small groups of "haves" and very large numbers of "have nots." With few exceptions, this is exactly how the world has worked until quite recently: a relatively small group of people using a large portion of the population to build and expand their own wealth and power.

In some parts of the world, benevolent leaders created societies where human dignity and fairness were valued, and democratic forms of government later evolved. In other places, however, such a transformation required violence, followed by constant vigilance to protect freedoms won. Which brings us to America.

After a bloody revolution and unlikely victory, we won our freedom . . . at least some of us did. Only one time since the Revolutionary War have we shed blood to preserve the nation. Ironically, it was for the sole purpose of denying freedom to slaves and to preserve the wealth of plantation owners. Those rich white Southerners far outnumbered their poor white neighbors. So, how did they persuade those who had so little to fight on their behalf? They simply convinced them that the North was attempting to deny them their way of life, that freed slaves would take their jobs and possibly do them harm. Sound familiar? It comes right out of a playbook that is still being used today—the politics of division.

The good news is this: the Founding Fathers *did* leave us with a form of government that allows for peaceful change, and there have been pivotal points in our nation's history where this has occurred, despite dirty political tricks, deceit, and outright corruption by those with bad intent. In each instance, the oppressed had to become so marginalized, so abused, and so fed up that they rose up in defiance.

Who are these people? They are the very soul of this nation. They don't expect too much out of life. They are happy to play their role, so long as they can maintain some form of dignity and provide for their families. They are not greedy or overly ambitious. They shun politics. In many ways, they often enjoy life more than those who have great wealth. They are normal, pragmatic people, focused on solving problems, not getting caught up in political ideology. They often remain silent until they are robbed of their humanity or their ability to provide for their families. These are the circumstances in which we find ourselves today.

For the greater part of our existence, this nation has been controlled by two parties, each with agendas crafted by political extremists. There is little appetite for compromise between them, and, as a result, the gap between the haves and have nots is widening. As sad as it seems, this is only a part of the problem. Slavery still haunts us today. Outright enslavement and subsequent segregation have been replaced by systemic racism, ugly in all its forms.

Racism continues to keep people of color from receiving good educations, owning homes, and building wealth. You would think a shrinking white middle class might be motivated to stand in solidarity with their fellow black Americans, but well-funded politicians are using unlimited resources to sow the seeds of division. Many poor rural Americans are content to live in poverty, so long as they are allowed to own plenty of guns, maintain their religious freedoms—which *are not* being threatened—and sit superior in their own minds over people who do not look like them. These are not good people, but they are Americans, and they do vote. The only way you, the "frustrated majority," can lessen their influence is to get involved in the political process, or, at the very least, go out and vote. Of course, not all poor, rural white Americans fit this profile, but enough of them do to form a potent political voting bloc.

Before we go any further, let me explain who comprises America's frustrated majority. They, for lack of a better word, are "normal." I'm not being sarcastic, and, at the end of this book, I will explain what I think it means to be a "normal," pragmatic American. It's not what you might think.

To continue, we are approaching a point where even the most politically complacent should be willing to rise up and force the extreme left and far right to moderate their positions, to promote the best interests of the nation as a whole. It's time we ask ourselves: *What kind of country do we want to live in?* That's what this book is about. Before we can ask that question, we need to get a clear view of what America looks like at this moment in time.

This book does not contain elaborate political arguments. It's a straightforward, common-sense call to political arms, written in plain language. It's a call for a "non-violent" revolution . . . while that is still possible. With each passing year, more and more is being taken away from hard-working Americans. The top one percent pay a fraction of the taxes they once did, if they pay any at all. Many large corporations pay not a penny in federal income tax.

If the American way is to survive, the frustrated majority must get involved. Admittedly, a group of unorganized activists can do little against the powers of the Republican and Democratic parties. What's needed is a third party.

For now, we have to deal with the parties we have; this is not an ideal situation. Republicans are guilty of showering the wealthy with unearned tax breaks and businesses with corporate welfare. Democrats will condemn the cost of health-care and then gladly accept contributions from insurance and pharmaceutical companies.[1]

This book is designed to cut through the massive disinformation campaign being waged by big business and its enablers in congress. The goal here is to present a set of facts, along with a starting point for a course of action that might correct what has become a massive imbalance of power and wealth. Throughout the book, great pains have been taken to back up and attribute all assertions with unbiased sources. I say "unbiased," but these sources most certainly have agendas, and that is to do things differently from how they are currently being done. So, of course, the old political guard is going to question their motives.

One last thing before we commence: the title of the book. *Common Sense* was a political pamphlet written by Thomas Paine in 1776. Its contents have been studied by countless historians since. Yet, Wikipedia probably provides the most straightforward description of its purpose:

> *"Writing in clear and persuasive prose, Paine marshaled moral and political arguments to encourage common people in the Colonies to fight for egalitarian government."*

Am I arrogant to think I can pick up where he left off? Clearly, I am no one special. A former TV reporter, now public relations professional, I am just another citizen. But guess what? When he wrote *Common Sense*, Thomas Paine was no one of real consequence. I am an American just like you, and I've had enough. I just hope the words in this book can spark the passions of those who, for too long, have remained silent. You know, the "frustrated majority." Maybe you are among them. If so, just remember: you don't have to do everything—just do *something*. Together, maybe we can make this country what we all hope it can be.

★

One

WHY READ THIS BOOK?

Although *Common Sense 2.0* is well researched, it is not an academic essay. This is a populist publication, aimed at provoking action. Each of the following chapters focuses on specific areas within public policy where greed, neglect, and outright corruption have created massive inequality.

It's a lot to take in. Policy can be dry and a bit overwhelming. On top of that, we live in a world plagued by information overload. So often, we see something disturbing on the news, and then politicians lining up to point fingers and assign blame. That's what American politics has been reduced to—playing the blame game. In reality, there's plenty of blame to go around. Both Republicans and Democrats are complicit to varying degrees, but the GOP is, by far, most responsible for our nation's raging inequalities, concentration of wealth, and decimation of the middle class.

I have no doubt that there are still some moderate Republicans who are capable of reason and can be swayed to compromise, but, for now, the party itself is too deeply aligned with wealthy special interests to be of much use. A number of Democrats, though well intentioned, seem to be fixated on some type of purity test, seeking to determine who is the most "woke." In the process, they are dividing the party at a time when it most needs to be united, not to mention alienating independents they should be trying to engage. Then, there are those in both parties who put their re-elections ahead of all else. While I do harbor some hope for the Democratic party, the best thing we can do now is to establish a viable third party—more on that later.

Most Americans could care less about politics. They want practical solutions. But here's the thing: if you want things to get better, you've got be part of the solution. You must get informed and involved. With the avalanche of information on the web, it's hard to keep all the pertinent issues straight. On that note, I hope this book will provide some clarity, context, and perspective. We must fully absorb the magnitude and source of our nation's troubles before we can begin taking action.

When you're finished reading this little book, I pray you will find that most of us have a lot in common. Yes, we're all different—that's what *should* make America great—but, make no mistake: we, the frustrated majority, also share common enemies whose greed knows no bounds. They know they cannot possibly defeat us if we stand together; that's why they are hell-bent on dividing us.

So, let's stand together! First, let's examine our most pressing issues. The next 12 chapters will outline just how our leaders have failed to address wage stagnation, taxation, corporate gluttony, healthcare, defense spending, racial justice, voter suppression, education, and political chicanery. In the end, we consider a possible solution. Clearly, this is not the America most of us want, but if we come to terms with our current reality and pull together, it can become the nation we hope it can be.

★

Two

BUILDING A NATION
ON PRINCIPLES AND OPPRESSION

D ON'T GET ME WRONG. AMERICA, when it lives up to its
highest ideals, is a beautiful thing. As citizens, it's our
responsibility to seek a more perfect union. Too often, however,
we have missed the mark. We need to be honest. We don't practice
what we preach, at least in terms of equality. In fact, much of
the wealth this nation now possesses was built upon the backs
of people we oppressed. None of us had anything to do with it,
but we should at least come to terms with this.

"America" and "freedom" are two words deeply intertwined.
Since the dawn of our nation, freedom has been enshrined in the
American lexicon—it defines what it means to be an American.
On one hand, freedom evokes feelings of pride and patriotism,
and that's a good thing. On the other, it has also been used to
promote "rugged individualism." Some Americans believe that
"freedom," in its most perfect state, means the right to pursue our
lives unencumbered by government interference. It's a nostalgic

notion. If you work hard enough, and the government stays out of the way, you can achieve whatever you set out to do, which sounds great. We all would like to believe it's true, but it's based on the premise that once people "make it," they will do the right thing—they'll do what's best for their country. I would submit that, while that does happen on occasion, it's the exception, not the rule. I know that sounds a bit cynical, but stay with me on this. You'll see where I'm going.

To paraphrase a familiar quote, some people are born on home plate and act as if they'd hit a home run. Yet, there are many, many more who never even got a chance to bat. Let's go back to the early 19th century. We were an agrarian society. Small farmers could provide for themselves and their families. Large landowners, most notably those with slave labor, did much better. This politically powerful class launched generations of wealthy Americans whose station in life was assured by birth, not effort. This marked the beginning of a societal pattern that would precede nearly every major advance made by our nation. In each instance, greater wealth and power was accumulated by exploiting other people. It started with slavery. Then, as the nation grew, settlers moved westward, each time claiming land and displacing Native Americans. This is not meant to be a white guilt trip. It happened. There's nothing that can be done to change it, but it did set in motion a series of actions, and we need to acknowledge that there was serious collateral damage.

Moving ahead to the post-Civil War era, the absence of slave labor fueled innovation, and new inventions ushered in the Industrial Revolution, allowing machinery to do the jobs once reserved for men. Those machines, however, did not run themselves. Work in the factories was unpleasant, dangerous, and low-paying. Who better to do that work than immigrants pouring into America seeking better lives? Many of them never found it, but their descendants did. Yet again, the nation took another giant leap forward, built on the backs of the oppressed. These people, including children, worked six to seven days a week, 15–18 hours a day, in sweat shops for minuscule wages.[1]

Where was the American government in all of this? For the poor and suffering, nowhere to be found. Many of the nation's political leaders were becoming wealthy themselves, often for turning a blind eye as large corporations, then called "trusts," colluded to stifle competition and depress wages. Then, on September 6, 1901, an assassin shot President William McKinley. That singular event, while tragic, precipitated a substantial change in government and the distribution of wealth. The new president, Theodore Roosevelt, set in motion actions that represent the first shift toward breaking up corporate monopolies and establishing a more even, competitive playing field.

In 1906, Upton Sinclair published his seminal work *The Jungle*, a book which cast light on the poor sanitation and working conditions within the meatpacking industry.[2] This marked the beginning of what would become the modern labor movement. Over the course of the next several decades, unions organized, and public opinion began to influence legislation. One event was especially impactful. In 1911, the Triangle Shirtwaist Company in New York's garment district caught fire. Locked doors and inadequate fire exits trapped workers inside, leading to 146 deaths. That signaled a call for action. Organizations like the National Consumers League launched public-information campaigns to inform consumers *where* and *how* their clothes were made, giving *them* the choice to buy from manufacturers that provided fair wages and decent working conditions. Franklin D. Roosevelt's New Deal legislation and Fair Labor Standards Act of 1938, along with its subsequent amendments, provided for a minimum wage, a 44-hour work week, the elimination of child labor, protections for unions, and workplace safety standards.[3] This represented the first serious attempt to build the kind of America where everyone had a fair shot. Well, not exactly everyone.

After World War II, the GI Bill allowed certain veterans to pursue an education, own a home, and build wealth, giving them a ticket to the middle class. Yet, that opportunity was denied to most black veterans.[4] Despite these gross inequities, the America that emerged over the next three decades may have come as close as we have ever come to becoming the nation we thought we might be. That in no way condones the horrible treatment of black Americans, but it was a step in the right direction. Then, we took a *big* step back.

The election of President Ronald Reagan in 1980 launched a massive shift in wealth across the nation. Large tax cuts for the wealthy never created the trickle-down effect that was promised. Instead, budget deficits and a soaring national debt grew by the year. Corporate welfare favored large companies over small ones, and defense spending soared. Yes, we won the Cold War, but at a great price. One administration after another began charging things to the nation's credit card without concern for the consequences.

Year by year, healthcare became more expensive, as did the lifesaving prescription drugs that would be developed. What's more, government support for public colleges and universities dwindled, putting a college degree out of reach for many. Those who do go to college are often saddled with crushing debt. And that's just one of the casualties linked to decades of tax cuts and loopholes for the rich. When there's not enough tax money coming in, spending cuts follow. The nation's infrastructure is crumbling from decades of neglect. Teachers are chronically underpaid. And while the Defense Department always seems to have enough money to purchase the latest weapons systems, there never seems to be enough left to help veterans returning home who are missing limbs and suffering from PTSD.

The top one percent and corporate America, however, are doing quite well, thank you. Record earnings and a soaring stock market have led to a massive concentration of wealth that has, in reality, created *two Americas*. How bad is it? You're about to find out. Many of us think we know something about each issue, but looked at collectively, and in detail, it's absolutely staggering.

Three

WAGE STAGNATION AND THE HIGH COST OF LOW LIVING

IN THE EARLY 1980s, the American people were robbed, and the thievery continues to this very day. It began when President Ronald Reagan, with the support of both Republicans and Democrats, initiated the first in a series of tax cuts to benefit wealthy individuals and large corporations.[1] Why would Democrats participate in such a thing? Consider this: they had just lost the presidency, and the economy was stymied by high interest rates, inflation, and stagnant growth. The preferences of the voting public were beginning to change. Republican operatives saw an opportunity to widen the base of their party, luring frustrated Democrats over to their side. To do that, they had to create a new narrative. So, they set out to convince certain groups of Americans that they shared a common enemy.

One group ripe for attack: Labor unions. The GOP cited unions' unreasonable demands as a major reason for America's *economic* decline. Next up, *moral* decline. Republicans pledged to reverse *Roe vs. Wade* and bring prayer back into the classroom. Finally, they stirred up gun owners, taking a hard line against any attempts to limit gun ownership. No matter how reasonable such a change might be, they claimed that any limitation whatsoever created a slippery slope, leading to an outright ban of private firearms ownership. In a relatively short period of time, these issues began to resonate, and a new political alliance was struck, a tacit agreement: You let us keep our money, and we'll let you keep your guns, fight to reverse *Roe vs. Wade*, and stand squarely behind the fundamentalist Christian movement.

Four decades later, abortion is still legal, though some states have passed new restrictive laws destined to be challenged in the Supreme Court.[2] And guns are more plentiful than ever. There are an estimated 400 million of them in the United States, more than one for every man, woman, and child.[3] As for union membership: in the 1960s, nearly one-third of American workers belonged to a union. Today, it's about one in ten.[4] Now, if we're going to be intellectually honest, we should admit that union demands—and corruption—had become excessive, but rather than push for reform, an all-out effort ensued to limit their influence. The consequences of those actions have been particularly harmful to the middle class.

Writing for *The New Yorker*, Caleb Crain states, "Whenever the rate of unionization in America has risen in the past hundred years, the top one percent's portion of the national income has tended to shrink. After Roosevelt signed the Wagner Act and other pro-union legislation, a generation of workers shared deeply in the nation's prosperity. Real wages doubled in the two decades following the Second World War, and, by 1959, Vice-President Richard Nixon was able to boast to Nikita Khrushchev that 'the

United States comes closest to the ideal of prosperity for all in a classless society.'" [5]

Wage Theft

With union membership and wages on the decline, where did all that money go? During the past three decades, people in the top 0.1 percent have enjoyed a significant gain in their income. Those on the other end of the socioeconomic spectrum, not so much. Reporting for CBS News, business reporter Alain Sherter found that, between 1980 and 2014, income for the middle 40 percent of American households—meaning those with average earnings of $65,300—rose a total of 42 percent. That's about 1.2 percentage points annually. By comparison, income for the top one percent—people with an average income of $1.3 million—rose 204 percent, or 6.0 percent per year. For the top 0.1 percent ($6 million in average income), income jumped 320 percent. And for the wealthiest of the wealthy, the top .001 percent (average income of $121.9 million), income shot up 636 percent, or nearly 19 percent per year. [6]

In her report, Sherter quotes Gabriel Zucman, one of the country's leading experts on inequality, who said, "The U.S. economy is broken. Since 1980, there has been no growth for half of the population (the bottom 50 percent of income earners) and only very limited growth for the bottom 90 percent, while a tiny minority (the top one percent) has seen its income skyrocket." In a report he co-authored, Zucman found that the average annual income for people in the bottom 50 percent had gone nowhere, stuck around $16,000. [7]

A recent analysis by the Brookings Institution revealed that 53 million workers ages 18 to 64—or 44 percent of all workers—earn barely enough to live on, averaging about $18,000 per year.

These low-wage workers' occupations include retail sales, cooks, food/beverage servers, janitors/housekeepers, personal care/service workers, and various administrative positions. Having a low unemployment rate is not worth much when so many jobs pay so little. Critics will say these jobs are held primarily by young people or secondary earners in their households. The data shows otherwise:

★ Two-thirds of low-wage workers are in their prime working years of 25 to 54.

★ More than half work full-time, year-round.

★ Roughly half are primary earners or contribute substantially to family living expenses.

★ Thirty-seven percent have children, of whom 23 percent live below the federal poverty line.

★ Just fewer than half are low-wage workers aged 18 to 24 who are in school or already have a college degree.[8]

Another study by the Economic Policy Institute discovered large gaps by gender, race, and education level. "Rising wage inequality and slow and uneven hourly wage growth for the vast majority of workers have been defining features of the U.S. labor market for the last four decades, despite steady productivity growth," said EPI Senior Economist Elise Gould, who authored the report. "But these alarming trends are not inevitable—they are a direct result of a series of policy decisions that have reduced the economic power of most workers to achieve faster wage growth." Here are some additional findings from her report:

★ Most workers experienced consistent positive wage growth in only 10 of the last 40 years.

★ Wages for the bottom 50 percent of college graduates are lower today than they were in 2000.

★ Wage growth for low-wage workers in states with minimum-wage increases was much faster than in states without minimum-wage increases between 2018 and 2019. The 10th percentile wage rose by 4.1 percent in states with minimum-wage increases, compared to just 0.9% growth in states without minimum-wage increases.

★ Black-white wage gaps remain significantly wider now (14.9 percent) than in 2000 (10.2 percent).[9]

"Wage growth for low- and middle-wage workers continues to be slower than would be expected in an economy with relatively low unemployment," said Gould. "Given this sluggish wage growth, policymakers should not presume that the economy has already achieved full employment. Instead, policymakers should take steps to foster strong wage growth, such as raising the federal minimum wage, addressing pay disparities, and protecting and strengthening workers' rights to bargain collectively for higher wages and benefits."[10]

A Declining Standard of Living

Each day, more Americans are waking up to a new reality. They are discovering what it's like to live among the nation's poor and struggling. They are the growing lower economic class who scrounge for scraps while they watch the top one percent live high on the hog. Many have gone from well-paying jobs to earning minimum wage, their once-decent standard of living now just a memory.

If you don't know what it's like to live like this, here's a glimpse: the Economic Policy Institute and the National Low Income Housing Coalition report that a minimum-wage worker now needs 2.5 full-time jobs to afford a one-bedroom apartment in most of the United States. They found the national housing wage necessary for a modest one-bedroom apartment to be $17.90/hour.[11] The federal minimum wage has been stuck at $7.25 since 2009, the longest stretch of time without an increase since the minimum wage was first enacted. Here are some other things about the minimum wage you might want to know:

★ While some states have raised their minimum wages, 21 are still stuck at the $7.25 mark, many with laws that prevent local governments from going any higher.

★ These 21 states are home to 56 million workers, while a total of nearly 100 million people live in states with minimum wages that are less than $15/hour.

★ Since 2009, the real value of the federal minimum wage has eroded and is now worth $6.11/hour in today's dollars.

★ Of the 10 states with the highest concentration of African Americans, eight are frozen at $7.25/hour.

★ Polls show overwhelming support for raising the national minimum wage to $15/hour.[12]

Imagine what it's like to be stuck earning the same hourly wage, year after year, as the price of everything goes up. Sure, inflation has been low, but over time, it all adds up.

According to the Bureau of Labor Statistics Consumer Price Index Inflation calculator, $100 had the same buying power in 1980 as about $332 has today. Here's what's happened to the price of some basic household items during the past four decades:[13]

PRODUCT/SERVICE	1980	2020
Bacon	1.453/lb.	5.505/lb.
Bananas	0.319/lb.	0.570/lb.
Flour	0.203/lb.	0.438/lb.
Oranges	0.339/lb.	1.244/lb.
Tomatoes	0.703/lb.	2.221/lb.
Electricity	0.053/KWH	0.134/KWH
Regular Unleaded Gasoline	1.10/Gal.	2.631/Gal.

Yet, these increases are minuscule compared to the cost of housing, transportation, healthcare, and education:

PRODUCT/SERVICE	1980	2020
Average Price of a Home[14]	$64,000	$327,100
Buick Regal	$6,925[15]	$27,920[16]
College Tuition, Room/ Board***	$3,101[17]	$23,091 (2016–17)[18]

As for healthcare, insurance premiums have gone sky high, completely out of reach for those living paycheck to paycheck. Take a look at the 2019 Employer Health Benefits Survey from the Kaiser Family Foundation (KFF).[19]

Average Annual Premiums for Single and Family Coverage, 1999-2019

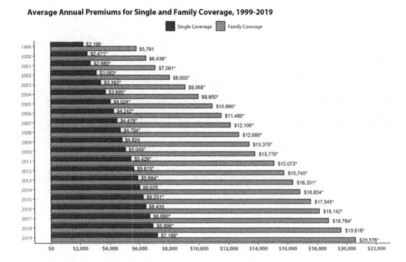

FIGURE 1.10 *Average Annual Premiums for Single and Family Coverage, 1999–2019*

Between 1999 and 2019, average annual health-insurance premiums have risen from $2,196 for individuals and $5,791 for families to $7,188 for individuals and $20,578 for families. That's an increase of 286 percent. Moreover, KFF found the list prices for most top Medicare Part D drugs increased as much as nine times the rate of inflation between 2016 and 2017.[20]

And when you spend that much money on housing, transportation, education, and healthcare, there's not much left for food. According to Feeding America, hunger is a growing problem. Here are the numbers before the Coronavirus ravaged the U.S. economy:

★ More than 38 million people are living in poverty in America. In 2019, most of their families earned less than $25,750 per year.

★ More than 37 million people struggle with food insecurity in the United States, including up to 11 million children.

★ Children are more likely to face food insecurity than any other group in the United States.[21]

How did we allow all this to spin so far out of control? How much more do the Republican and Democratic parties think we will take? The great American scholar Clay Jenkinson said it better than I ever could:

> *"I have watched in my short lifetime as the American rich have gotten much, much, much richer and the poor continue to struggle to survive, and the middle class has shrunk dramatically and lost ground. I have watched as the CEOs of the great corporations have rewarded themselves at astronomical figures until the average American CEO now earns 224 times than the average median worker of that same corporation. And I simply don't believe it, that the CEO deserves to earn on average $13.4 million per year, while most of his employees live paycheck to paycheck and wonder how they are going to send their children to college. I openly and passionately resent that fewer than one percent of the American people now own 95 percent of the wealth of America. This is not acceptable. This is not right. This is not morally justifiable. And, this is not sustainable."[22]*

★

Four

TAXES ARE FOR
THE LITTLE PEOPLE

Y OU'VE PROBABLY HEARD IT SAID that nothing in life is certain except death and taxes. For most Americans, that is true, but not for America's top one percent. Okay, even they can't escape death, but they do, on average, live longer, given their access to high-quality healthcare. As for taxes, here's one thing that is certain: America's wealthiest citizens pay far less than they should.

Without question, taxation is a complicated topic. The tax code is a tangled web of rules and regulations, and I think it's that way by design. If you were trying to make it hard for the average American to avoid paying their taxes, wouldn't it make sense to create a system so complicated that only a highly specialized CPA or lawyer could make sense of it?

Some critics have tried to pull back the curtain on this system, seemingly bent toward inequity, but with only limited success. Conservatives attack them as socialists and liberals. And to that,

I say, "Of course, they do." These people, and the organizations they represent, are trying to crash the party. Personally, I prefer the word "progressive" over "liberal," which simply means we seek to better the nation as a whole, not just for the privileged.

Four decades of regressive taxation has done a lot of damage. Our national debt is more than $26 trillion—not because government spends too much, but because it spends money in all the wrong places and fails to adequately tax the rich. Since 1980, conservatives have claimed that cutting taxes for the wealthy and large corporations causes a trickle-down effect, yet there is zero evidence to suggest this has occurred in any meaningful way. Let's look at what *has* happened.

Top Marginal Tax Rate vs. Effective Tax Rate
With federal income taxes, there's often a big difference between the top marginal tax rate and the effective rate, and the number of brackets has varied greatly through the years. Since 1963, the top bracket has dropped from 91 percent to 37 percent in 2018, with a single-year decrease in 1988 to a mere 28 percent.[1]

YEAR	TOP MARGINAL TAX RATE	YEAR	TOP MARGINAL TAX RATE	YEAR	TOP MARGINAL TAX RATE
1963	91.00%	1971	70.00%	1993	39.60%
1964	77.00%	1981	69.13%	2001	39.10%
1965	70.00%	1982	50.00%	2002	38.60%
1968	75.25%	1987	38.50%	2003	35.00%
1969	77.00%	1988	28.00%	2013	39.60%
1970	71.75%	1991	31.00%	2018	37.00%

This tells only part of the story and does not begin to describe what the wealthy really pay. Yes, there are plenty of deductions and tax loopholes, but let's stay with those tax brackets for now. Currently, there are seven of them, but there used to be a lot more, and the top .01 percent once paid a much higher rate than those who were just "somewhat" wealthy.[2]

2020 U.S. Tax Brackets

TAX RATE	SINGLE	MARRIED, FILING JOINTLY	MARRIED, FILING SEPARATELY	HEAD OF HOUSEHOLD
10%	$0 to $9,875	$0 to $19,750	$0 to $9,875	$0 to $14,100
12%	$9,876 to $40,125	$19,751 to $80,250	$9,876 to $40,125	$14,101 to $53,700
22%	$40,126 to $85,525	$80,251 to $171,050	$40,126 to $85,525	$53,701 to $85,500
24%	$85,526 to $163,300	$171,051 to $326,600	$85,526 to $163,300	$85,501 to $163,300
32%	$163,301 to $207,350	$326,601 to $414,700	$163,301 to $207,350	$163,301 to $207,350
35%	$207,351 to $518,400	$414,701 to $622,050	$207,351 to $311,025	$207,351 to $518,400
37%	$518,401 or more	$622,051 or more	$311,026 or more	$518,401 or more

Just look at the chart and think about the effect of those lowered rates, all the uncollected tax dollars. Those who make $1 million a year, $10 million a year, $100 million a year, and so on, are taxed at the same rate as those making $518,401 to $622,051. Now, think about all that money over the decades, invested, and subject only to a modest capital-gains tax of roughly 15 percent. That wealth builds up, money that could have been used for education, infrastructure, or simply put back in your own pockets. Instead, it accumulates, and the rich begin to make more money *from* their money than they do from their exorbitant CEO salaries. Not surprisingly, each year, the number of American billionaires grows at an astonishing rate.

A recent study by University of California at Berkeley economist Gabriel Zucman reveals that the 400 richest Americans—the top 0.00025 percent of the population—have tripled their share of the nation's wealth since the early 1980s. Combined, they possess more wealth than the bottom 60 percent of the country—150 million adults—who saw their wealth plummet from 5.7 percent in 1987 to 2.1 percent in 2014, a level of wealth inequality not seen since the Roaring Twenties. In fact, Zucman believes these numbers are understated, since many wealthy Americans hide assets in offshore tax shelters.[3]

What's more, Zucman found that America's top 10 percent own 70 percent of the nation's wealth, more than double the bottom 90 percent. In fact, he believes the division of America's wealth more closely resembles that of Russia and China than it does more-comparable democratic governments such as France and the United Kingdom. In a study co-written with fellow economist Emmanuel Saez, also of UC-Berkeley, they found that America's billionaire class actually has a lower effective tax rate than the working class. In "The Triumph of Injustice," they wrote that the 400 richest families paid a rate of 23 percent, compared to 24.2 percent for the bottom half of America's households. In comparison, the effective tax rate—what the rich really paid after deductions and loopholes—was 47 percent in 1980 and as high as 56 percent in 1960.[4]

Much of this was reported by Christopher Ingraham of the *Washington Post* in 2019. In his article, Ingraham wrote that this wealth is used to perpetuate the system that created it, stating, "Our electoral system is highly dependent on outside financing, creating numerous opportunities for the wealthy to convert their money into influence and tip the political scales in their favor. As a result, politicians have become accustomed to paying close attention to the interests of the wealthy and enacting policies that reflect them, even in cases where public opinion is strongly trending in the opposite direction." Translation: when it comes to matters of the pocketbook, if you don't have a lot of money, many of your elected officials are not going to listen.[5]

So how did congress make this bad situation worse? In 2017, Donald Trump teamed up with Republicans to drop the average effective tax rate for the top 0.1 by another 2.5 percent and further reduced corporate tax rates.[6] Sure, they threw the middle class a bone, once the rich had carved away all the prime cuts for themselves.

Corporate Overlords

So, if wealthy individuals can "contribute" their way into paying lower taxes, imagine what even wealthier corporations can do. Not surprisingly, they are also paying a much-smaller share of federal tax revenue. According to Americans for Tax Fairness, their portion dropped from one-third in the 1950s to one-tenth today. Some pay little or nothing at all. For example:

★ General Electric, Boeing, Verizon, and 23 other profitable Fortune 500 firms paid no federal income taxes from 2008 to 2012.

★ 288 large and profitable Fortune 500 corporations paid an average effective federal tax rate of just 19.4% from 2008 to 2012.

★ U.S. corporations dodged $90 billion a year in income taxes by shifting profits to subsidiaries, often no more than post office boxes, in tax havens.

★ U.S. corporations officially hold $2.1 trillion in profits offshore that have not yet been taxed here.[7]

And guess what? That was before Trump's 2017 tax bill. Since then, the Institute on Taxation and Economic Policy reports that, in 2018, 60 of America's biggest corporations paid nothing in federal income taxes on $79 billion in U.S. pretax income. Terrible, right? Hang on to your hat. Not only did they pay no taxes—they received tax rebates of $4.3 billion. Here are some select examples:

★ **International Business Machines (IBM)** earned $500 million in U.S. income and received a federal income tax rebate of $342 million.

★ **Amazon** reported $11 billion of U.S. income and claimed a federal income tax rebate of $129 million.

★ **Netflix** paid no federal income tax on $856 million of U.S. income.

★ **Molson Coors** reported $1.3 billion of U.S. income in 2018 and received a federal income tax rebate of $22.9 million.

★ **General Motors** reported a negative tax rate on $4.3 billion of income.

Here's a list of all 60 companies that paid no federal taxes in 2018:

1. Activision Blizzard
2. AECOM Technology
3. Alaska Air Group
4. Amazon.com
5. Ameren
6. American Electric Power
7. Aramark
8. Arrow Electronics
9. Arthur Gallagher
10. Atmos Energy
11. Avis Budget Group
12. Celanese
13. Chevron
14. Cliffs Natural Resources
15. CMS Energy
16. Deere
17. Delta Air Lines
18. Devon Energy
19. Dominion Resources
20. DTE Energy
21. Duke Energy
22. Eli Lilly
23. EOG Resources
24. FirstEnergy
25. Gannett
26. General Motors
27. Goodyear Tire & Rubber
28. Halliburton
29. Honeywell International
30. IBM
31. JetBlue Airways
32. Kinder Morgan
33. MDU Resources
34. MGM Resorts International
35. Molson Coors
36. Netflix
37. Occidental Petroleum
38. Owens Corning
39. Penske Automotive Group
40. Performance Food Group
41. Pioneer Natural Resources
42. Pitney Bowes
43. PPL
44. Principal Financial
45. Prudential Financial
46. Public Service Enterprise Group
47. PulteGroup
48. Realogy
49. Rockwell Collins
50. Ryder System
51. Salesforce.com
52. SpartanNash
53. SPX
54. Tech Data
55. Trinity Industries
56. UGI
57. United States Steel
58. Whirlpool
59. Wisconsin Energy
60. Xcel Energy[8]

Do you find this a bit shocking? Sorry to say, we are just getting started. Not only do these companies escape many of their tax burdens, they actually receive corporate welfare as "incentives" to expand and invest in new ventures, as if they would have just sat back and watched a competitor capture a new market as they stuffed all their cash reserves into a savings account.

★

Five

CORPORATE CODDLING, BUSINESS BLACKMAIL

YOU'VE SEEN IT IN THE NEWS MANY TIMES: a new company coming to town or an existing one expanding, followed by the words "tax incentives." Increasingly, that's the tool many cities and states use to lure or retain employers. Corporations know politicians score political points with these announcements, and they take full advantage, sucking away enormous amounts of money from local and state governments, thereby reducing their tax burdens to the lowest possible level.

Whether it's a manufacturer, a developer, or a professional sports team, they all know how the game is played. Developers convince municipalities to subsidize their projects with parking garages, infrastructure, and tax breaks to erect all sorts of venues and commercial endeavors. For a while, conference and convention centers were big cash cows, despite credible evidence indicating that these investments would not pay off . . . for the cities, that is. Developers cleaned up.

In many ways, doing business in America is now about coaxing the government into sweetening the bottom line. Maybe business schools should start teaching classes with titles like "Bellying Up to the Public Bar" or "Legal Extortion: A Smorgasbord of Options." Yes, there's never been a better time for America's most powerful corporations.

Before Theodore Roosevelt started breaking up the trusts and unions began securing workers' rights, the government did just one thing to help big businesses . . . they left them alone to do as they pleased, oftentimes with politicians enriching themselves in the process. Today, federal, state, and local governments fancy themselves as partners, all in the name of job growth and economic development, but at what cost? Each tax dollar forgiven must be accounted for. Proponents of these incentives say those dollars are recovered through economic growth, but like trickle-down economics, that rarely seems to happen. Ultimately, what follows are municipal budget cuts, working-class citizens paying higher taxes, more government debt, or any combination of the three.

Picking Winners and Losers

America is supposed to be about free markets, a moderately regulated capitalist nation, but when some companies receive subsidies and tax incentives and others don't, it creates an uneven playing field, fostering corruption and erosion of public trust. Human nature being what it is, you can understand why politicians love these governmental gifts. Bringing in new companies or promoting expansion earns big points with voters, keeping them in office. Of course, they can't grant these incentives all by themselves. In the Cato Institute's Handbook for Policymakers, Chris Edwards writes about the practice of "logrolling," whereby lawmakers bundle bills with specific earmarks for one another's pet projects. Everyone wins, except you and me. "Congress often enacts ill-conceived laws that benefit narrow groups at the expense of most citizens," says Edwards. "Many federal programs harm the overall economy, and they are only sustained because interest groups support them . . . Nearly all the spending in the $4 trillion budget stems from huge bills that bundle together many diverse provisions. Members of congress have neither the time nor the incentive to rigorously critique individual programs in these large bills. So, there is little debate about the real value of most federal spending."[1]

Federal Tax Incentives, Subsidies, and Bailouts

In 2015, Philip Mattera and Kasia Tarczynska issued a report, "Uncle Sam's Favorite Corporations—Identifying the Large Companies That Dominate Federal Subsidies," which revealed that the U.S. government had awarded $68 billion in grants and special tax credits to businesses during the prior 15 years, with two-thirds of that going to large corporations. Six of those companies received $1 billion or more, 21 got $500 million or more, and 98 took in $100 million or more. This does not include the hundreds of billions of dollars in loans, loan guarantees, and bailout assistance. The report also revealed that some of the corporations receiving these juicy deals are also dodging taxes by reincorporating abroad or merging with foreign companies. For instance, power equipment producer Eaton, which incorporated in Ireland but is based in Ohio, got $31.9 million, and oilfield services provider McDermott International, which incorporated in Panama but is based in Texas, received $12 million.

Government contractors really rake it in. While they bid on the roughly $400 billion spent each year by federal agencies in procuring goods and services, Mattera and Tarczynska found that nearly half of the 100 largest contractors also received federal subsidies. Among them, 30 have received loans, loan guarantees, and/or bailout assistance. Topping the list: General Electric, which received $836 million. Some other notable companies include United Technologies, Boeing, Lockheed Martin, Honeywell, and Raytheon.

It should be mentioned that these 11 companies, among the 50 largest recipients of federal grants and tax credits, are also among the top recipients of state and local subsidies:

* Boeing   * Lockheed Martin

* Dow Chemical   * NRG Energy

* Ford Motor Company   * Sempra Energy

* General Electric   * SolarCity

* General Motors   * United Technologies[2]

* JPMorgan Chase

State and Local
When it comes to incentives offered by the states, it's like the wild, wild west. We're talking a high-stakes poker game with states throwing everything they can at large employers to induce them to build, relocate, or expand. This competition, pitting states against each other, is not healthy for any of them or for the nation as a whole. "Programs and policies that affect interstate commerce are exactly the kind of manipulation of

trade between the states that the Framers of the Constitution wanted to prevent," said James M. Hohman, director of fiscal policy at the Mackinac Center for Public Policy in an op-ed for *The Hill*.

Hohman says these practices continue even though most people are opposed to them. "Progressives don't like the transfers of wealth to wealthy business owners," he says. "Conservatives don't like having everyone's taxes given to the political elite. Libertarians don't like interference in the economy. And pragmatists decry the waste and ineffectiveness."[3]

In their article "New Data on State and Local Incentives Across the U.S." in *Princeton Economics*, Cailin Slattery of Columbia Business School and Owen Zidar of Princeton University found that business tax incentives offered by state and local governments have tripled since the 1990s. They estimate that state and municipalities spend at least $30 billion a year on such incentives, but they consider that number to be a low-end estimate, citing other research methods that suggest the real number could be as much as $45 billion a year.

The competition is so fierce that some states have offered incentives that actually exceed the corporate revenues generated by the employer. Slattery and Zidar cite Nevada, South Dakota, Texas, Washington, and Wyoming, which have gained zero corporate income tax revenue but spend about $44 a year for each one of its citizens on incentives. And here's the thing: It's questionable how much that money really buys. They found that, in 2014, 670,000 employers established new locations, creating more than *5 million new jobs*. That same year, states gave $6.9 billion in incentives to 48 employers that promised only *50,000 jobs*. They also found that poorer areas pay a lot more in incentives on a per-job basis to lure and retain employers. Counties with an average wage of less than $40,000 pay more than $400,000 per job while those with average wages greater than $100,000 pay less than $100,000.[4]

How far will state and local governments go in this bidding war? How hard will employers push to squeeze them dry? Let's look at some examples.

Amazon

In 2018, Amazon was considering Loudoun County, Virginia, for its next data center. Despite being one of the wealthiest counties in the nation, the state designated the targeted property as an "opportunity zone," which allowed the awarding of tax breaks for companies that invest in "economically distressed" communities. The state submitted the plan to the U.S. Treasury Department for approval, and the contract was signed the following month.[5] A year later, Virginia approved a package of up to $750 million in state business tax incentives in exchange for Amazon building its HQ2 in Arlington.[6]

Apple

On the verge of bankruptcy in 1997, Apple struck a deal to keep its headquarters in Cupertino, California. In exchange, it would get half of the city's share of sales tax revenue generated by the company's sales to businesses in California for a minimum of five years. Reporting for the *Bloomberg Daily Tax Report*, Laura Mahoney found that, while Apple is now the world's most valuable company, it's still getting sales-tax rebates, according to a city official. Shockingly, she reports that the amount of money Apple has received over the years is kept confidential.[7]

The State of California

On September 12, 2019, the *Los Angeles Times* editorial board issued a scathing editorial calling out the state's localities for participating in a tax-break bidding war which it estimated cost local residents about $1 billion a year. Here's an excerpt:

> *"Cities agree to generous tax-sharing agreements to persuade companies to build warehouses or sales offices in their jurisdictions, rather than locating somewhere else. These agreements allow companies to keep a sizable chunk—in some cases more than half—of the local portion of the sales tax revenue attributed to the facility. That's money that could have been spent on public safety, street repairs, affordable housing, and other government services . . .*
>
> *"Why would local governments agree to forfeit so much money? Because California law allows retailers to attribute the sales taxes they collect from online purchasers anywhere in the state to the jurisdiction where their warehouse or sales office is located, not to the cities where the buyers live. A warehouse for a big online retailer can thus bring with it not just jobs, but also far more sales-tax revenue than a brick-and-mortar retailer that's just selling locally. A city council may be happy to part with more than half of that revenue, considering how much it would still collect."* [8]

Boeing

In 2013, the Washington State Legislature passed an $8.7 billion tax incentive package to encourage Boeing to remain in Washington and grow jobs in the state's aerospace industry. Why would the state pay such an exorbitant amount? Speaking on *The Daily Show with Trevor Noah* on March 18, 2019, Governor Jay Inslee put it this way: "If you've ever been mugged, you understand what it feels like. I was not happy with the Boeing situation because what happens is these corporations put a gun to your ribs and say, 'You're going to lose 20,000 jobs unless we get a tax break." While Boeing did keep its promise to build a new wing factory and the new 777 in Washington, its total employment dropped by 12,100 between 2013 and 2018.[9]

In an op-ed for *Business Insider*, Paul Constant, a fellow at Civic Ventures in Seattle, writes, "Our corporations have grown lazy and entitled, and they're taking advantage of the system, with no plan to ever pay us back. It's time to kick corporations off welfare for good."[10] To that, I say "Amen."

★

Six

AMERICAN HEALTHCARE: IN NEED OF A CURE

DEFENDERS OF AMERICA'S HEALTHCARE SYSTEM say we have the best healthcare in the world. It sounds good. You want to believe it's true, but it's really not. To be great, it would have to include everyone, which it most certainly does not. Most people seem to understand this—except the people who make our laws and control the nation's wealth.

A 2017 Gallup poll showed that 71 percent of Americans believed the U.S. healthcare system was in a state of crisis or had major problems, about the same percentage of people that held the view seven years prior, just before the passage of the Affordable Care Act.[1] Since 2017, little has changed, and major healthcare reform still seems unattainable.

Healthcare is like every other problem we face. A vast majority of people agree that there is something wrong, and most blame the other party or, in the case of independents and apolitical types, both parties. Regardless, there is plenty of blame to go around, and with each party dug in deep, there's little chance of compromise, which is probably for the best, since neither of them seem prepared to do what needs to be done. For now, healthcare in America is expensive, produces modest outcomes, and is somewhat corrupt.

The High Cost of Getting Well

The United States spends more money on healthcare than any other nation on Earth. In a study conducted by the Harvard T.H. Chan School of Public Health, the Harvard Global Health Institute, and the London School of Economics, researchers compared the United States with 10 other high-income countries—the United Kingdom, Canada, Germany, Australia, Japan, Sweden, France, Denmark, the Netherlands, and Switzerland—on approximately 100 key indicators that support healthcare spending.

In 2016, the U.S. spent 17.8 percent of its gross domestic product on healthcare, while the other countries ranged from 9.6 percent (Australia) to 12.4 percent (Switzerland). It should be noted that America has about 30 million people who are uninsured, while most people in the other countries are covered by health insurance. Factors contributing to America's costly system include:

★ Administrative Costs—8 percent of all U.S. healthcare spending is dedicated to activities related to planning, regulating, and managing health systems and services, compared to roughly 1 to 3 percent among the other countries.

★ Americans, on average, spent $1,443 per year on pharmaceuticals. The other nations ranged between $466 and

$939. For several commonly used brand-name drugs, the U.S. had substantially higher prices, often double the next-highest country.

★ The average salary for a general-practice physician in the U.S. was $218,173, compared to the other countries, where salaries ranged between $86,607 and $154,126.[2]

Let's take a closer look at actual dollars spent. According to data from Organisation for Economic Co-operation and Development (OECD), the United States spent $10,209 on healthcare per person in 2017, more than any other country among the OECD's 36 members. Here's how we rank, from top to bottom, on dollars spent:

1. United States—$10,209
2. Switzerland—$8,009
3. Luxembourg—$6,475
4. Norway—$6,351
5. Germany—$5,728
6. Sweden—$5,511
7. Ireland—$5,449
8. Austria—$5,440
9. Netherlands—$5,386
10. Denmark—$5,183
11. France—$4,902
12. Canada—$4,826
13. Belgium—$4,774
14. Japan—$4,717
15. Iceland—$4,581
16. Australia—$4,543
17. United Kingdom—$4,246
18. Finland—$4,173
19. New Zealand—$3,683
20. Italy—$3,542
21. Spain—$3,371[3]

Getting Less for More

Here is what makes no sense at all: we spend all that money and still produce less-favorable outcomes. In fact, we come up short in some key areas:

★ American life expectancy is the lowest among the 11 countries studied, at 78.8 years, with other nations ranging between 80.7 and 83.9.[4]

★ U.S. infant mortality was the highest, at 5.8 deaths per 1000 live births, versus a 3.6 per 1000 average for the other 11 countries.[5]

★ We have fewer doctors—just 2.4 practicing physicians per 1,000 people—well below the OECD average of 3.1.[6]

★ We have fewer hospital beds—just 2.6 per 1,000 people—lower than the OECD average of 3.4 beds.[7]

★ The average cost of hospital stays in the U.S. is 85 percent higher than the average for the other OECD countries—$18,000—compared to Canada, the Netherlands, and Japan, where stays range between $4,000 and $6,000 less.[8]

The Most Expensive Prescription Drugs on the Planet
Prescription drugs contribute mightily to the overall cost of healthcare, but that's just here in the United States. Unlike other nations, we do not regulate prices. In Europe, countries negotiate them, with excellent results. Even Medicare, America's only federally sponsored health insurance program, does not negotiate prices. Crazy, right? Why wouldn't we use our massive buying power as leverage? Just ask your congressman. Better yet, find out if she/he voted to prevent that. When prescription-drug benefits were added to Medicare in 2003, drug manufacturers successfully lobbied them to prohibit the federal government from using its huge purchasing power to negotiate drug prices.[9]

Those prices have soared in recent years. A U.S. House of Representatives Ways and Means Committee investigation found that, between 2011 and 2016, drug spending nationwide grew by 27 percent—more than 2.5 times the rate of growth in inflation. Pharmaceutical companies often claim higher prices fund research and development, but, far too often, they raise prices, sometimes dramatically, on drugs that have been around for decades.[10]

Gerard Anderson, professor of health policy and management at Johns Hopkins University, told NPR that research and development account for just 17 percent of total spending in most large drug companies. "Once a drug has been approved by the FDA, there are minimal additional research-and-development costs, so drug companies cannot justify price increases by claiming research-and-development costs," he said.[11]

The Big, Ugly Secret

Here's what the drug companies and their congressional puppets do not want you to know: in most cases, the companies selling the drugs never did the initial research to begin with. Instead, they bought patents from government-funded organizations like colleges and universities. A report from the Proceedings of the National Academy of Sciences revealed that NIH funding contributed to published research associated with every one of the 210 new drugs approved by the Food and Drug Administration from 2010 to 2016.[12] In an op-ed for *The Hill*, Jason Cone, Executive Director of Doctors Without Borders USA, wrote:

> *"If the public funds the research that led to the development of a certain medicine, there should be limits to what government will allow companies to charge consumers. It*

should be unacceptable for taxpayers to fund a new med-
icine that the public can't even afford to buy once it hits
the market. Early research on one of Swiss pharmaceutical
company Novartis' best-selling drugs, a cancer drug called
Gleevec (imatinib)—a truly life-changing medicine for
people with leukemia—was substantially funded by U.S.
taxpayers through National Institutes of Health grants and
support from the Leukemia Society."

Mr. Cone goes on to point out "that the pharmaceutical industry takes all the credit for developing the breakthrough gene-altering chimeric antigen receptor T-cell (CAR T) therapy—a therapy that can cost patients $475,000—even though the first two CAR T treatments for multiple myeloma came out of NIH-funded research."[13]

What We Pay, What Other Countries Pay

A Bloomberg analysis found that, even after discounts negotiated by insurers, many of the world's top prescription drugs cost far more in the U.S. And for those who lack insurance and have to pay out of pocket, the cost soars even higher. For instance, the cholesterol drug Crestor is $86.40 with the insurance-company discount but $216 without it. Here are some other top drugs and how each compare:[14]

COUNTRY	CRESTOR	LANTUS	ADVAIR	JANUVIA	SOVALDI	HUMIRA	HERCEPTIN	GLEEVEC
USA	$86.40	$186.38	$154.80	$268.61	$17,700	$2,504.50	$4,754.45	$10,122.30
Germany	$40.50	$60.90	$37.71	$39.00	$17,903.70	$1,749.26	$3,185.87	$3,003.30
Canada	$32.10	$67.00	$74.12	$68.10	$14,943.30	$1,164.32	NA	$2,420.70
China	$30.00	$139.30	$32.00	$18.00	NA	$1,070.57	$2,310.02	NA
Japan	$28.80	$64.40	$51.05	$47.40	$13,020	$980.34	$1,731.06	$2,205.60
UK	$25.50	$63.65	$46.99	$48.00	$16,770	$1,157.53	$2,678.36	$2,645.10
Norway	$20.09	$45.25	$24.28	$34.20	$13,462.20	$918.41	$2,169.99	$2,093.10
France	$19.80	$46.60	$34.52	$35.40	$16,088.40	$981.79	$2,527.97	$2,303.10
Australia	$8.70	$54.05	$29.28	$33.60	NA	$1,242.75	$3,141.84	$2,585.10

Footnote:
Crestor—Cholesterol-lowing pill
Lantus—Long-acting insulin
Advair—Asthma inhaler
Januvia—Diabetes pill
Sovaldi—Hepatitis C pill
Humira—Rheumatoid Arthritis self-injection
Herceptin—Breast cancer infusion
Gleevec—Chronic myeloid leukemia pill

According to the House Ways and Means report, the U.S. could save $49 billion annually on Medicare Part D alone by paying the average price for drugs charged to most other countries.[15]

A System Designed to Fail

These numbers can be a bit mind numbing, but what they symbolize is a system that just doesn't work. While people are rarely turned away at hospital emergency rooms, does that really matter? Just because hospitals treat the uninsured does not mean the system is working. According to the American Hospital Association, U.S. hospitals provided more than $660 billion in uncompensated care to their patients since 2000.[16] So yes, they got treated, but only after their health had deteriorated to a point that required hospitalization, where the cost of care is most expensive. Perhaps if they'd had health insurance and preventative care, those trips to the hospital would have been unnecessary.

Who pays for all this care? We do, through higher costs. So, we pay either way. Why not provide health insurance for everyone and do it more efficiently? Because health-insurance companies have a good thing going. They make lots of money, and they don't want to give it up. Lawmakers opposed to a single-payer system say that Americans don't want to lose the health insurance they love. You can almost see the insurance lobby's ventriloquist putting his hand in their backs, speaking the words for them. Just like the pharmaceutical industry, health-insurance companies make big political contributions to keep America's health-insurance system just as it is.

Do You Really Love Your Health Insurance?

To close this chapter, let's take a moment to consider the single-payer system. First off, it's not nationalized healthcare.

Providers would still be private. Single payer just takes the profit motive out of health insurance. Under a single-payer system, everyone would be insured, much of the cost funded by savings obtained by replacing today's inefficient, profit-oriented system, supplemented by modest new taxes based on income level. According to Physicians for a National Health Program, premiums would disappear, most households would save money, and patients would no longer face barriers to care such as copays and deductibles.[17]

Again, this is not socialized medicine. It's social insurance, like Medicare. And those people who *think* they have great private health insurance? Many of them discover it's not so great once they get sick. According to the National Patient Advocate Foundation, medical expenses contribute to 62 percent of bankruptcy cases in the United States, while one out of every five American families will struggle to pay a medical debt each year.[18] And that does not include the scores of people who have their credit completely destroyed. When you consider the insane monthly premiums, rising out-of-pocket expenses, and cutbacks in covered services, what's to like, let alone love, about our current system?

★

Seven

YES TO WAR, NO TO VETERANS

I HAVE TREMENDOUS RESPECT for our nation's military men and women, which is why I find the treatment they receive at the hands of our government so offensive. Politicians and top military brass are always saying "Nothing's too good for the troops," but they have an odd way of demonstrating it. The United States seems to have no reservations about sending them into battle. Afterwards, however, their concern seems to wane.

While there are times when military intervention is essential, so often it's just us meddling in another nation's affairs. Being the world's top cop is expensive. Every dollar we spend on defense is a dollar unavailable to educate a child, lift someone out of poverty, replace an aging bridge, and especially important, care for a disabled veteran.

Why do we spend so much? For one reason, there are people in congress who view the defense budget as a jobs program. Consider cutting a new weapons system, and the congressman who has that defense contractor in their district breaks out the heavy artillery in opposition. Another reason why we spend so much money: we deploy our military forces far more often than you may realize.

For a nation that claims it only seeks peace, we spend an inordinate amount of time engaged in armed conflict. Putting aside the American Revolution, as well as World Wars I and II—all clearly necessary for the formation and preservation of our country—we have spent most of our history engaged in military action. If you include the Cold War, America has been in a near-constant state of conflict since 1941. This fact sheet produced by the U.S. Department of Veterans Affairs lists all our *major* wars:

★ American Revolution (1775–1783)

★ War of 1812 (1812–1815)

★ Indian Wars (1817–1898)

★ Mexican War (1846–1848)

★ Civil War (1861–1865)

★ Spanish American War (1898–1902)

★ World War I (1917–1918)

★ World War II (1941–1945)

★ Korean War (1950–1953)

★ Vietnam War (1964–1975)

★ Desert Shield/Desert Storm (1990–1991)

★ Global War on Terror (October 2001–Present)[1]

Yet, this does not begin to illustrate how frequently we deploy our forces. Between 1948 and 1991, America engaged in military intervention 46 times, and with each passing year since, our leaders seem to find this easier to do. Between 1992 and 2017 alone, we deployed military troops another 188 times.[2] The most recent examples include Panama, Liberia, Bosnia, Haiti, Somalia, Croatia, Zaire, Sudan, and Macedonia.

The price tag for all these incursions? Currently, America's defense budget stands at $732 billion, dwarfing every other nation in the world. In fact, we spend more money than the next 10 nations combined. All told, defense accounts for 15 percent of all federal spending and about half of discretionary spending.[3]

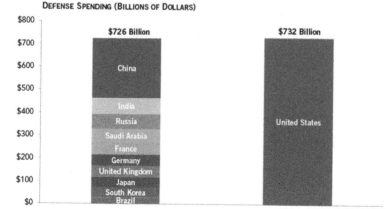

PETER G. PETERSON FOUNDATION — The United States spends more on defense than the next 10 countries combined

DEFENSE SPENDING (BILLIONS OF DOLLARS)

$726 Billion: China, India, Russia, Saudi Arabia, France, Germany, United Kingdom, Japan, South Korea, Brazil

$732 Billion: United States

SOURCE: Stockholm International Peace Research Institute, *SIPRI Military Expenditure Database,* April 2020.
NOTES: Figures are in U.S. dollars converted from local currencies using market exchange rates. Data for the United States are for fiscal year 2019, which ran from October 1, 2018 through September 30, 2019. Data for the other countries are for calendar year 2019. The source for this chart uses a definition of defense spending that is more broad than budget function 050 and defense discretionary spending.
© 2020 Peter G. Peterson Foundation   PGPF.ORG

The Military-Industrial Complex

In the final days of his presidency, Dwight Eisenhower addressed the nation in what is known as the "Military-Industrial Complex Speech." Though he had spent most of his adult life in uniform, Eisenhower had grave concerns about the expansion of the military, the production of weapons, and its implications for the nation. "In the councils of government, we must guard against the acquisition of unwarranted influence, whether sought or unsought, by the military-industrial complex," said Eisenhower. "The potential for the disastrous rise of misplaced power exists and will persist. We must never let the weight of this combination endanger our liberties or democratic processes. We should take nothing for granted. Only an alert and knowledgeable citizenry can compel the proper meshing of the huge industrial and military machinery of defense with our peaceful methods and goals, so that security and liberty may prosper together."[4]

Eisenhower foresaw a future of excessive spending and corruption coming our way, and he was right. Fraud in the defense industry is rampant. A Department of Defense (DoD) report to congress revealed that, between 2013 and 2017, there were 1,059 criminal cases of fraud, resulting in the conviction of 1,087 defendants, involving 409 businesses. All the while, the Pentagon entered into more than 15 million contracts with contractors who had been indicted, fined, and/or convicted of fraud, or who had reached settlement agreements. The total amount of those contracts was valued at more than $334 billion, according to the DoD report.[5]

Treatment of Vets

By its very nature, war produces death, but it also produces broken bodies and tormented minds. I'm about to write something that is going to seem outlandish, but stay with me. Groups like Wounded Warriors *should not exist*. Why? Because they should not be necessary. America sends its sons and daughters into harm's way with the understanding that, if anything happens to them, their care is assured. That is a lie. Do we provide care? Sure. Do we provide adequate care? Hardly. Perhaps our nation's leaders view our brave men and women as expendable. Does that sound harsh? The evidence is clearly damning.

Nuclear Guinea Pigs

In the early years of the nuclear age, the U.S. government used military servicemembers as guinea pigs to evaluate the effects of radiation following a nuclear detonation. Called Operation Desert Rock, it was a series of military tests in the 1950s designed to measure the effects of radiation on ground troops. More than 50,000 U.S. soldiers were exposed to 69 nuclear blasts.[6]

Chemical Guinea Pigs

Then, there was the secret government program to test mustard gas and other chemical agents on American troops. During World War II, 60,000 enlisted men, mostly black and Puerto Rican, as well as a number of Japanese Americans, participated in experiments that were cruel and barbaric. In an investigative report, National Public Radio (NPR) spoke with Rollins Edwards, an African-American soldier who was among the test subjects. "It felt like you were on fire," recalls Edwards, now 93 years old. "Guys started screaming and hollering and trying to break out," he said during the NPR interview. "And then some of the guys fainted. And finally, they opened the door and let us out."

For years, these men were unable to speak about what happened, threatened with dishonorable discharge and prison time if they did.[7] This, of course, kept them from seeking treatment at VA hospitals for the health issues. According to the Centers for Disease Control and Prevention, exposure to mustard gas can lead to respiratory diseases and blindness, and can increase the risk of lung and respiratory cancer.[8]

Agent Orange

Now, let's jump forward to the Vietnam War, where the military used Agent Orange to defoliate dense forests, which made it easier to spot enemy troops. There are mountains of credible research documenting the many health effects for troops exposed to this chemical, yet the VA typically reviews each of them one at a time, rather than conducting a more comprehensive study.

Some of the better reporting on this subject came from an investigative series published in 2016 by journalists Mike Hixenbaugh of *The Virginian-Pilot* and Charles Ornstein of *ProPublica*. One of the scientific experts they interviewed was Jeanne M. Stellman, an emeritus professor at Columbia University. A widely published Agent Orange researcher, she said, "For really almost 40 years, there has been a studious, concerted, planned effort to keep any study from being done and to discredit any study that has been done."[9] In that report, it was revealed that there were an estimated 2.6 million Vietnam veterans exposed to Agent Orange. Some now refer to the VA claims process as "Delay, deny, wait till I die."[10]

Many of the exposed are Navy and Air Force vets, whom the VA initially claimed could not have been affected because they were not on the ground. However, further research suggests runoff from rivers reached naval ships offshore, contaminating drinking water. Also exposed were airplane crews that sprayed the toxic herbicide. In the *Virginian-Pilot/ProPublica* report, one man was identified as a central figure in what is described as a coverup, Alvin L. Young, known as "Dr. Orange." A Pentagon consultant, it's reported he recommended "that Air Force officials quickly and discreetly chop up and melt down a fleet of C-123 aircraft once used to spray the chemical. The consultant also suggested how to downplay the risk if journalists began asking questions: "The longer this issue remains unresolved, the greater the likelihood of outside press reporting on yet another 'Agent Orange Controversy.'"[11] Even as Vietnam vets begin to die off, this problem is still not going away. Using data of 668,000 vets examined by the VA, Hixenbaugh and Ornstein found that the odds of exposed service members having a child born with birth defects are three times greater than that of the general public.[12]

Persian Gulf Syndrome

It seems the Agent Orange response is now standard procedure for the VA when dealing with former service members who can no longer serve. According to the Boston University School of Public Health, there are approximately 200,000 veterans from the 1991 Gulf War that continue to suffer from Gulf War Illness (GWI), a set of symptoms that includes chronic pain, fatigue, and memory impairment caused by sarin chemical warfare agent, pesticides, and pyridostigmine bromide (PB) pills meant to protect soldiers from nerve gas during deployment.[13]

And what has the VA done for these suffering veterans? According to the *Military Times*, during the first two quarters of fiscal 2015, it denied nearly 82 percent of claims filed by Gulf War veterans. In 2011, the denial rate was 76 percent. These low approval rates are a "complete contravention of 1998 laws passed to improve Gulf War veterans' ability to have their claims approved," wrote Veterans for Common Sense Director

Anthony Hardie in testimony before two House Veterans Affairs subcommittees. "If we measure VA's success by how it has approved Gulf War veterans' claims 25 years after the war, VA has failed most ill and suffering Gulf War veterans." Nearly 700,000 service members were deployed during the Gulf War. Of the nearly 55,000 claims filed for Gulf War Syndrome, only about a fifth were approved.[14]

The Real Cost of Military Action

How we spend the public's money says a lot about who we are as a nation. We enter wars and other military engagements often unprepared or unwilling to deal with the consequences. In recent years, we routinely hear stories about veterans waiting months, even years to get an appointment at a VA Care Center.[15] You know what's sad? All these incidents were eventually reported, but we have become a society of short attention spans. We move on. Media outlets know this. When they sense our interest is waning, they move on to other stories. We can do better as citizens. We need to stay focused and demand change. Our veterans deserve it.

★

Eight

AMERICA'S ORIGINAL SIN

AS A WHITE MAN, writing about race comes with all kinds of hazards. If time machines were real and someone approached me 30 years ago to describe race relations in 2020, I would be stupefied. How could it be? How could we have not found a way to evolve—or, at the very least, just get along?

Life is about choices. You can screw up, and, many times, the damage is repairable. Other times, transgressions comes with consequences that last a lifetime. What's true for people is also true for nations. For America, slavery is our original sin, and we are still feeling its repercussions.

I am encouraged that well-meaning but historically complacent white people are beginning to lend their voices to the cause of racial justice. Still, we have a long way to go. I would like to approach this sensitive topic with a passage from Dr. Martin Luther King, Jr., that I find especially relevant. In Dr. King's Letter from a Birmingham jail, he wrote:

I must confess that, over the past few years, I have been gravely disappointed with the white moderate. I have almost reached the regrettable conclusion that the Negro's great stumbling block in his stride toward freedom is not the White Citizens' Counciler or the Ku Klux Klanner, but the white moderate, who is more devoted to "order" than to justice; who prefers a negative peace, which is the absence of tension, to a positive peace, which is the presence of justice; who constantly says: "I agree with you in the goal you seek, but I cannot agree with your methods of direct action"; who paternalistically believes he can set the timetable for another man's freedom; who lives by a mythical concept of time and who constantly advises the Negro to wait for a "more convenient season." Shallow understanding from people of good will is more frustrating than absolute misunderstanding from people of ill will. Lukewarm acceptance is much more bewildering than outright rejection.[1]

You may think things are far better now than they were 50 or 60 years ago. With all due respect, a half century represents a very short period of time when viewing societal change. I would submit that current means of oppression are more subtle in some ways, but still quite overt in others. Case in point: police brutality. We will likely never know the full magnitude, the sheer level of terror inflicted on black people by bad cops, but we do know what's happening now. We have video evidence. People are beginning to open their eyes, so now is a good time to examine more closely what racism looks like in the 21st century. Spoiler alert: it goes way beyond police violence and touches nearly every aspect of life. Nonetheless, we'll start with the police.

Life and Death

According to the Proceedings of the National Academy of Sciences of the United States of America, our nation's cops kill far more people than police in other advanced industrial democracies, black Americans in particular. In fact, black men are about 2.5 times more likely to be killed by police over the course of their lives than white men. Specifically, about 1 in 1,000 black males will be killed by law enforcement. What's more, police use of force is responsible for 1.6 percent of all deaths involving black men between the ages of 20 and 24.[2]

It is now abundantly obvious that police treat black people much different from white people. Consider the issue of drug possession, specifically marijuana. According to the American Civil Liberties Union, marijuana arrests account for more than half of all drug arrests in the United States. Of the 8.2 million marijuana arrests between 2001 and 2010, 88 percent were for simple possession. And while white and black people use marijuana at similar rates, black people are 3.73 times more likely to be arrested.[3]

Once arrested, people of color are also more likely to go to prison. Research published by the Drug Policy Alliance shows that prosecutors are twice as likely to pursue mandatory minimum sentences for black people.[4] Moreover, black men in America receive prison sentences that are 19.1 percent longer than those of white men convicted for the same crimes.[5] And let's stop calling our prisons "correctional institutions." What's being corrected? Somebody gets busted with a joint. They go into prison an otherwise law-abiding citizen, and, after experiencing near-continuous violence behind bars, come out a hardened criminal. How sad and stupid is that?

Systemic Racism

We've been hearing a lot about systemic racism. The words sound almost cryptic. As a white man, I cannot begin to grasp it completely, myself. What I do know is that it's a form of racism deeply embedded in our societal structure that uses insidious methods to erect barriers and remove options for people of color. I can only imagine how angry I would be if I were forced to navigate life under such circumstances. When your options are taken away, it feels like your life is no longer your own. Want to know what that's like? Take a look:

Health

★ Black women are three to four times more likely to die during childbirth.[6]

★ Black babies are nearly 2.5 times more likely to die before their first birthday.[7]

★ Death rates for black Americans surpass those of Americans overall for heart disease, cancer, diabetes, and HIV.[8]

★ White males live approximately seven years longer than African-American males, and white women live more than five years longer than black women.[9]

Employment

★ Black people are twice as likely to be unemployed; once they are employed, they earn nearly 25 percent less than white people working the same job.[10]

★ Resumes with white-sounding names receive 50 percent more callbacks than those with black names.[11]

★ Black workers are less likely to be employed in jobs consistent with their level of education.[12]

★ The U.S. poverty rate is 7.0 percent for white men, 20 percent for black women, and 18 percent for Latinas.[13]

Wealth

★ The average white family has 41 times more wealth than a black family and 22 times more than a Latino family.[14]

★ The percentage of black families with zero or negative wealth rose by 8.5 percent to 37 percent between 1983 and 2016.[15]

★ White families hold 90 percent of the nation's wealth, Hispanic families hold 2.3 percent, and black families hold 2.6 percent.[16]

Education

A good education is a great way to improve your life. For many people of color, that is easier said than done. Since the Supreme Court ruled school segregation unconstitutional in 1954 (*Brown v. Board of Education*), there has been some improvement, yet the majority of America's children still attend racially concentrated school systems, and black-majority schools do not receive anything approaching equal funding.

A report from nonprofit EdBuild finds that nonwhite schools received $23 billion less than white school systems in 2016. It's also reported that 20 percent of all students are enrolled in districts that are both poor and nonwhite, but just five percent live in white districts that are financially challenged. Moreover, for every student enrolled, the average nonwhite school district receives $2,226 less than its white counterpart.[17]

Home Ownership
Now if you're black and you do manage to make a little money, you'll probably want to buy a house. Once again, easier said than done. Let's use the City of Chicago as an example. Until the federal government outlawed it, banks would avoid lending in black neighborhoods, a practice called "redlining." While it is now "technically" illegal, you'd hardly know it. A report by WBEZ and City Bureau found major disparities in the amount of money lent in white neighborhoods versus black and Latino. Reporters examined records for all home-purchase loans reported to the federal government between 2012 and 2018—168,859 of them combined, totaling $57.4 billion. Here's what they found:

★ 68.1 percent of dollars loaned went to majority-white neighborhoods, while just 8.1 percent went to majority-black neighborhoods and 8.7 percent to Latino neighborhoods. Put another way, for every dollar the banks loaned in Chicago's white neighborhoods, they invested just 12 cents in black neighborhoods and 13 cents in Latino neighborhoods.

★ Gaps in home-purchase lending were even wider among some of the city's largest lenders. JPMorgan Chase lent 41 times more money in white neighborhoods than in black ones. Bank of America: 29 times more money in white communities than in black communities and 21 times more than in Latino neighborhoods. Wells Fargo: 10 times more to white areas than black and 17 times more than Latino.

★ In one neighborhood alone, Chase had two branches with deposits totaling $80 million but made only 23 home-purchase loans there over the course of seven years.

The primary way many American families build wealth—and pass it down—is through home ownership. Without fair lending practices, homes in black and Latino neighborhoods don't sell, often sitting vacant. Businesses move out. Home values go down and fall into disrepair, which banks use as a rationale to deny loans. It's a vicious cycle.[18]

The Season of Hate

Earlier in the book, we touched on the politics of division, whereby powerful interests create bogeymen—people you can blame for all your troubles. This tactic is being used with great regularity, and we are seeing far too many angry white people—a minority, yet sizable group—pointing their collective fingers at their fellow citizens. They've been getting stirred up for a while now, but their anger has hit new heights since Donald Trump got elected. You can see it in the headlines and in the rising number of hate crimes. In 2016, the FBI recorded 6,121 such criminal incidents, 6,063 of which were motivated by:

★ Racial and ethnic bias (57.5 percent)

★ Religious bias (21.0 percent)

* Sexual-orientation bias (17.7 percent)[19]

By 2018, that number increased to 7,036 incidents and 8,646 victims, classified by:

* Racial and ethnic bias (59.6 percent)

* Religious bias (18.7 percent)

* Sexual-orientation bias (16.7 percent)[20]

So, I have a question for my white readers: If you had to endure a life such as this—the discrimination, systemic poverty, police brutality, mass incarceration, lack of opportunity—wouldn't you be mad? I know I would. During the protests and riots that followed the murder of George Floyd, activist Kimberly Jones made a video that went viral. In it, she described how America built its wealth on the backs of slaves, and then, in freedom, continued to deny black people the rights and dignity of equal citizens. While not a violent person herself, it's clear that she fully understands why so many people want to burn down buildings when police officers commit murder. I will close out this chapter with her final words on the matter.

"Far as I'm concerned, they could burn this bitch to the ground, and it still wouldn't be enough. And they are lucky that what black people are looking for is equality and not revenge!" [21]

★

Nine

SUPPRESSING THE VOTE

O F ALL THE RIGHTS WE POSSESS IN THIS COUNTRY,
the right to vote is perhaps the one we hold most
sacred. In theory, it keeps elected officials accountable to
the *public*, not special interests. We, however, do not live in
a theoretical world, which explains why both parties have,
at times, expended great amounts of energy to suppress this
right. This chapter will come across as a direct attack on the
Republican Party, but that's only because the GOP has been
using the tools of suppression to great effectiveness for the
past couple of decades. That's not an opinion. It's a statement
of fact. Since the 2000 election, Republicans have been on
a crusade to manipulate the voting process in their favor.
They've done so by suppressing specific groups of voters,
redrawing congressional districts, and spending money at
unprecedented levels.

Stopping the Vote

Suppressing voters is a nasty business. Its history goes back to America's failed attempt at Reconstruction. Under the neglectful eye of President Andrew Johnson, states throughout the South engaged in the most appalling forms of discrimination to ensure that former slaves could not exercise their newly acquired rights. During the next nine decades, white southerners and the Democratic Party—which controlled the South during that time—erected one roadblock after another to keep these Americans away from the ballot box.

The tactics used were varied and many, including poll taxes, literacy tests, and other forms of assessments that required black voters to explain complex aspects of the U.S. Constitution, various legal statutes, and anything else they could dream up. In one instance, a Mississippi registrar required black voters to state how many bubbles were contained in a bar of soap.[1] If such methods failed to do the job, violence often followed. During Reconstruction alone, it's estimated that at least 2,000 freed slaves—men, women, and children—were victims of terror lynchings.[2]

Now, you're probably thinking, *This happened a long time ago, and such things no longer occur.* Yes, the more-overt forms of violence are less frequent—that is true. But the Republican Party has a whole new boxful of tools that skirt the spirit of our laws and produce the same chilling effect.

While there have been many instances of localized forms of voter suppression throughout history, we'll stick with some more recent examples. Let's begin with Florida during the 2000 presidential election. An investigation by the U.S. Commission on Civil Rights found widespread voter disenfranchisement that produced a very close result and sealed George W. Bush's victory in the national presidential race. The report found that, in most instances, black voters were the primary target. Among the Commission's findings:

* Black voters were nearly 10 times more likely than non-black voters to have their ballots rejected.

* While only 11 percent of Florida voters were African American, they cast about 54 percent of the 180,000 spoiled ballots throughout the state.

* Counties with large minority populations were more likely to possess voting systems with higher spoilage rates than the more-affluent counties with significant white populations.

The report also revealed that the state's "overzealous efforts to purge voters from the rolls, conducted under the guise of an anti-fraud campaign, resulted in the inexcusable and patently unjust removal of disproportionate numbers of African-American voters from Florida's voter registration rolls for the November 2000 election." In Miami-Dade County alone, more than 65 percent of the purged voters were African American, yet they represented only 20.4 percent of the population.

When these voters tried to cast their ballots, poll workers attempted to contact voting officials but were unable to reach them. Citing specific examples, investigators noted a poll worker in Palm Beach County who "testified that she had to use her personal cell phone to attempt to contact the election supervisor's office. Despite trying all day, she got through only two or three times over the course of 12 hours." Also included in the report, "A Broward County poll worker testified that, in past elections, it took about 10 minutes to get through to the elections supervisor. During the November 2000 election, she turned away approximately 40-50 potential voters because she could not access the supervisor of elections."[3]

That same year, the St. Louis City Board of Elections illegally purged 49,589 eligible voters from the active-voter rolls. Republican officials were claiming rampant voter fraud, yet they could not substantiate their claims. According to the Brennan Center for Justice, "The allegations yielded only six substantiated cases of Missouri votes cast by ineligible voters, knowingly or unknowingly, except for those votes permitted by court order. The six cases were double votes by four voters—two across state lines and two within Missouri—amounting to an overall rate of 0.0003%."[4]

After the 2000 election, Republicans began refining their craft, evading the spirit of America's voting laws. Then, in 2013, everything changed. Rigging elections got a whole lot easier. In *Shelby County v. Holder*, the U.S. Supreme Court gutted two provisions of the Voting Rights Act of 1965, opening the floodgates for states to return to the bad old days. States that had previously been monitored for infractions (based on a history of violations) were no longer under the federal government's watchful eye.[5] What followed was a highly orchestrated effort to:

★ Purge Voting Rolls

★ Pass New Voter ID Laws

★ Redraw Congressional Districts

Purging Voters

Certain Republicans would have you believe that the reason they purge voting rolls is to eliminate voters who have died or moved to another address. If that were all they were really trying to accomplish, it would be like using a shotgun to kill an ant. Essentially, citizens were getting kicked off the voting rolls because they hadn't voted during the past few elections. Republicans knew that a large percentage of these targeted voters were black. They sat out elections not because they're unpatriotic. They stayed home because they had been made to feel that their votes did not matter, as they saw their rights questioned at every turn. If you think these are isolated instances, let's take a trip around the country.

★ While serving as Georgia's Secretary of State, Brian Kemp, now the Governor, disenfranchised a lot of voters. On a single day in July 2017, his office removed 560,000 of them because they'd "skipped one too many elections." An American Public Media investigation estimated 107,000 of the people purged under the policy would have otherwise been eligible to vote.[6]

★ According to *The Atlanta Constitution-Journal*, since 2012, Georgia has removed about 1.4 million people from the voting rolls, most of them because they stopped participating in elections.[7] They never gave up their right to vote—they just failed to vote in recent elections.

★ In Ohio, the vast majority of the 158,000 voters purged in 2019 were still eligible to vote.[8]

★ In April 2019, Oklahoma removed more than 88,000 voters for inactivity.[9]

★ Until very recently, another tool used to purge voters was called Interstate Crosscheck, which was an alliance of 28 states created to identify voters who were registered in more than one state. However, it was later revealed that the system had an error rate of approximately 99 percent.[10]

Did any of these actions prevent voter fraud? Of course not, because it's not a real problem. In fact, law professor Justin Levitt conducted a study that showed that, out of one billion votes cast nationwide from 2000 to 2014, only 31 involved voter impersonation.[11]

Voter-ID Laws

Voter-ID laws seem harmless enough. Requiring an ID to vote? What's the big deal? Dig deeper, and it becomes clear. It's just another tool used to disenfranchise certain voters.

There are many ways to establish your identity when you go to the polls. Until recently, Georgia accepted forms of identification that included utility bills, bank statements, and private employer IDs. In 2005, the state eliminated those and many others. The intent was clear . . . make it harder for black people to vote. Now, voters in a growing number of states are required to present either a driver's license or a state-issued ID to cast a ballot.[12] Typically, these are issued at states' departments of motor vehicles, often called DMVs. Regardless, it's estimated that up to 11 percent of American citizens do not possess either form of identification.[13] Many of them are poor and/or minorities. You might think that getting these IDs would not be all that difficult, but that depends on where you live.

When attorneys for the U.S. Department of Justice took a map of Georgia and overlaid locations for the state's department of Drivers Services (DDS), there were five times as many black households (versus white) located in counties without a single DDS office. In fact, only about one-third of the state's counties even *had* a DDS office.[14] Let's take another trip around the country and look at some other examples:

★ In Indiana, 60 percent of applicants seeking a license were turned away by the state's Bureau of Motor Vehicles because they lacked the proper documents. Most notably, they needed a birth certificate. How's this for political chicanery? In Marion County, where more than 200,000 of the state's black population resides, the Health Department requires a driver's license to get a copy of a birth certificate.[15]

★ When Alabama passed a photo-ID law in 2014, it refused to include public-housing IDs, which are issued by the government.[16]

★ When Texas passed its voter-ID law that effectively made a driver's license the primary form of ID, a lawsuit ensued, claiming the law put a heavy burden on minorities. During the trial, one judge noted that some voters would have to travel up to 120 miles to obtain an ID. The state's defense? Traveling far distances was a "reality of life of choosing to live in that part of Texas."[17]

★ Texas allows voters to present a handgun license to vote but not a student ID from a state university. More than 80 percent of handgun licenses issued to Texans in 2018 went to white people, while more than half of the students in the University of Texas system are minorities.[18]

★ During the 2016 election, North Carolina voters faced mass poll closures. In 40 counties with large black communities, citizens had 158 fewer early-polling places where they could cast their votes.[19]

★ In Wisconsin, one former Republican staffer made clear the real objective of voter-ID laws. Testifying in a federal trial, Todd Allbaugh said that GOP senators were "giddy" about the idea that Wisconsin's voter-ID law might keep Democrats, most notably minorities, from voting. "They were politically frothing at the mouth," he said.[20]

Gerrymandering

Gerrymandering is an odd word that describes a form of legal corruption, if there is such a thing. It allows the party in power to redraw congressional maps to create an unfair advantage.[21] Historically, both parties have done this, but during the past couple of decades, Republicans have turned the practice into a science. Using data analytics, they can surgically slice up neighborhoods to cram as many Democratic voters as possible into a small number of districts, leaving the remainder solidly in the Republican column. Looking at some of the resulting maps, you can see just how sinister this is.

North Carolina is among the worst offenders. Even though Democrats comprise more than 50 percent of registered voters, Republicans maintain a dominant 10-3 seat advantage. How could that be? Much of that can be credited to the late Thomas Hofeller, a former Republican operative who turned gerrymandering into a mad science.

In an investigative report by *The New Yorker*, reporter David Daley explained how Hofeller's mapmaking prowess changed North Carolina from a 7-6 congressional majority to a GOP stronghold. He began by creating spreadsheets full of data, detailing every relevant demographic such as age, party affiliation,

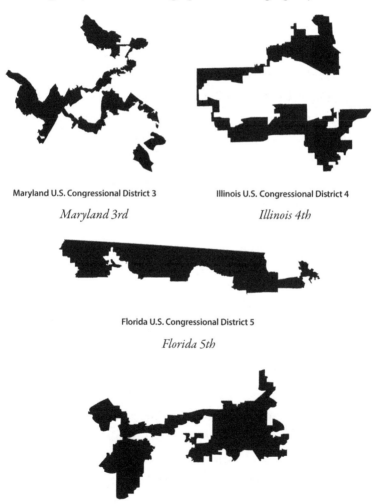

Maryland U.S. Congressional District 3

Maryland 3rd

Illinois U.S. Congressional District 4

Illinois 4th

Florida U.S. Congressional District 5

Florida 5th

Texas U.S. Congressional District 33

Texas 33rd

sex, and so on. He even compiled a list of 5,429 North Carolina college students who appeared to lack the proper ID to vote. He created maps with titles like "Greensboro Master Race," which contained a color-coded map showing the city's black population, age eighteen and older, by precinct. He had spreadsheets that detailed racial minorities who lacked driver's licenses. In his report, Daley writes:

> *"Hofeller wrote to a Republican attorney about an effort to match North Carolina's master voter-registration file against the driver's-license base to see which voters might be affected by the I.D. law. The team also looked to compare that information against that of the closest Department of Motor Vehicles offices. 'After the addresses are standardized and geo-coded for all three files, the next step will be a determination of the distance from each voter address to both the nearest DMV office and nearest in-county early voter center,'"* Hofeller wrote on February 4, 2014.[22]

North Carolina Republicans acknowledge the maps *do* discriminate, but on the basis of partisanship, not race. Certainly, such a process subverts the spirit of democracy. Before he died, Hofeller trained other Republican operatives around the nation, and his work has impacted congressional delegations in Texas, Arizona, Mississippi, Alabama, Florida, and Virginia.[23]

We are now left with a system that values partisan purity above all else, and the spirit of compromise is its greatest victim. God help the Republican who grows a conscience and deviates in any way from the far-right agenda. Party extremists will quickly put forth another candidate to take them out in the next primary. Just ask Eric Cantor. The former House Majority

Leader had solid conservative credentials, but when he moderated some of his views, that was all it took. He lost in the primary to a Tea Party candidate. One last time, let's take a quick trip around the country to look at the damage gerrymandering leaves in its wake:

* In 2016, two Georgia Republican members of the General Assembly barely won re-election when the number of black residents began to increase in their districts. The solution? The legislature simply redrew the district maps and put the black neighborhoods in a nearby Democratic district.[24]

* After the 2010 census, Texas had 4.3 million new residents, mostly black and Hispanic, but by cleverly altering the maps, Republicans received three out of the four new districts awarded to the state. A federal district court later blocked the move.[25]

* When Republicans gained control of the Wisconsin legislature, they redrew maps and gained a significant advantage.[26] In 2012, despite receiving a majority of the votes, Democrats captured only 39 percent of the seats in the general assembly.[27]

Money, Money, and Money

As you can see, our democracy is being manipulated. None of it happens without money. In fact, you might say that the three most important elements for winning an election are money, money, and money. And that's just plain sad. You could have the best ideas in the world and the best intentions, but if you run for office and lack the financial resources, you will most likely be squashed like a bug.

The greatest blow to democracy occurred in 2010, when the Supreme Court ruled in *Citizens United v. Federal Election Commission*, opening up the financial floodgates. Essentially, this ruling created a whole new legal landscape where money spent by corporations and special-interest groups for political purposes is considered free speech. Therefore, they can spend as much as they want, so long as they don't exceed limits for individual candidates. They can, however, spend unlimited money on a candidate's *behalf*. Super PACS are now running roughshod over our political process, spreading all kinds of misinformation, completely unregulated.

According to the Brennan Center for Justice, "Super PAC money started influencing elections almost immediately after *Citizens United*. From 2010 to 2018, Super PACs spent approximately $2.9 billion on federal elections. Notably, the bulk of that money comes from just a few wealthy individual donors. In the 2018 election cycle, for example, the top 100 donors to Super PACs contributed nearly 78 percent of all Super PAC spending." Surveys show that 94 percent of Americans believe that money is the source of our political dysfunction, and, yet, nothing seems to change.[28]

If you're among the frustrated majority but have not jumped into the fight, time is running out. It is every bit as bad as it seems. You cannot look away. You must insert yourself into the political process, even if it's just to make a small contribution of time and/or money. Your vote still trumps their money . . . for now. Before long, democracy may slip through our fingers, and a *peaceful* revolution may no longer be possible.

★

Ten

AN EDUCATION SYSTEM
STRIVING FOR MEDIOCRITY

TRY GOOGLING "INSPIRATIONAL EDUCATION QUOTES," and you'll find plenty of sentimental passages lauding the virtues of teachers and learning. Every one of them is true. A good education *can* take you far. Yet, it's not always easy to come by, unless, of course, you are wealthy. Then, you're in good shape. The rest of America, not so much.

Sure, there are plenty of good public schools, but they're often located in high-dollar zip codes. Taken collectively, America's public schools are not making the grade. For now, there's only so much the federal government can do to improve the situation. That's because America has always allowed states and localities to control K-12 education.

Each community has its own sets of challenges, but it all comes down to money. Poor school districts have less money, and wealthy ones have more. The results are predictable. Only

11 states take a more progressive approach, supplementing resources in poorer schools. For the other 39, the gaps in spending can be rather large. For instance, New York spends about $12,400 more per student annually than Idaho.

There are those who say that you cannot just throw money at a problem. In some instances, that is true—but not when it comes to education. According to the Center for American Progress, student scores on the National Assessment of Educational Progress (NAEP) are directly correlated with per-pupil spending. Funding impacts all aspects of the student experience. Consider the air quality and temperature inside many of America's crumbling schools. Both can negatively affect student learning. More than half of U.S. public schools are in need of repair. Most importantly, well-funded schools can offer smaller classes, recruit better teachers, and provide more one-on-one support as well as mental-health counseling for students at risk.[1]

Student Performance

When comparing test scores, some states do much better than others. In 2015, for instance, there was a nearly 30 percentile point difference in math-proficiency rates between the top and bottom states.[2] As a whole, the numbers are discouraging. Scores from the NAEP, widely known as "the nation's report card," show:

4th-Grade Proficiency

★ Math—41% students proficient

★ Reading—35% students proficient

8th-Grade Proficiency

★ Math—34% students proficient

★ Reading—34% students proficient

And on the ACT, 36 percent of test takers did not meet *any* of the four benchmarks. According to the Center for Education Reform, the percentages of graduates meeting the ACT College Readiness Benchmarks in math and English are the lowest they've been in 15 years.[3]

So, how does this compare with other nations around the world? According to the Program for International Student Assessment (PISA), the United States ranks 37th in math among these countries:

1. B-S-J-Z (China)
2. Singapore
3. Macau (China)
4. Hong Kong (China)
5. Chinese Taipei
6. Japan
7. Korea, Republic of
8. Estonia
9. Netherlands
10. Poland
11. Switzerland
12. Canada
13. Denmark
14. Slovenia
15. Belgium
16. Finland
17. Sweden
18. United Kingdom
19. Norway
20. Germany
21. Ireland
22. Czech Republic
23. Austria
24. Latvia
25. France
26. Iceland
27. New Zealand
28. Portugal
29. Australia
30. Russian Federation
31. Italy
32. Slovak Republic

33. Luxembourg   36. Hungary
34. Spain   37. **United States**[4]
35. Lithuania

For the two other major categories, the United States ranks 13th in reading and 18th in science.[5] How could we lag so far behind? We are the world's largest economy, the leaders of the free world, right? Like any problem, it's no one thing, but poverty, race, curriculum, and funding are the major contributing factors.

Poverty

Nearly one in six American children live in poverty. That's roughly 12 million of our most vulnerable souls. Almost half live in *extreme* poverty. Nearly 73 percent are children of color. According to the Children's Defense Fund, poverty tops 25 percent among:

★ Black children in 35 states and the District of Columbia

★ Hispanic children in 29 states

★ American Indian/Native Alaska children in 20 states.

There are only two states where poverty rates for white children are 20 percent or higher.[6]

Poverty can have a dramatic effect on student learning. In a column for *Philanthropy News Digest*, Kent McGuire, President and CEO of the Southern Education Foundation, wrote, "A student who is hungry or cannot see or hear adequately is likely to have problems concentrating in class. We also know that children from low-income families have much higher rates of untreated dental conditions and endure more acute illnesses that lead to chronic absenteeism and lost instructional time. If education-reform policies are insensitive to these realities, there is little reason to expect that learning outcomes for low-income children will improve."[7]

Racial Justice and Education

If our nation ever hopes to defeat racial injustice, we must correct inequities in the education system. We touched on this in a previous chapter, but let's go a little deeper. According to the United Negro College Fund:

* African-American students are less likely to have access to college-readiness courses. Only 57 percent have access to the full range of math and science courses necessary for college readiness, compared to 81 percent for Asian-American students and 71 percent for white students.

* African-American students are often located in schools with a greater concentration of novice teachers, who receive lower salaries.

* 1.6 million students attend schools with sworn law-enforcement officers but no school counselor.

* The average reading score for white students on the National Assessment of Educational Progress (NAEP) 4th- and 8th-grade exam is 26 points higher than for black students. Similar gaps are seen in math.

★ The 12th-grade assessment also reveals alarming disparities, with only seven percent of black students performing at or above proficient on the math exam, compared to 32 percent for white students.[8]

These children of color are every bit as smart as the other students, but they cannot keep pace without proper resources. Among developed countries, America's overall education system is now mediocre. Is it too much to ask that children of color receive an education that, at the very least, meets that minimal standard?

Investing in Our Children's Future

Money may not buy happiness, but it can produce a better educational system. A study published in the *Quarterly Journal of Economics* estimates that the "effect of a 21.7% increase in per-pupil spending throughout all 12 school-age years for low-income children is large enough to eliminate the education-attainment gap between children from low-income and non-poor families." Researchers found this level of investment produced an approximately 20-percentage-point increase in graduation rates and an additional year of educational attainment. Increasing spending as little as 10 percent still made a significant difference, elevating the high school graduation rate by 7 percent for all students and by about 10 percentage points for low-income students."[9]

Any increase in spending should include more money for teachers. According to the Center for American Progress, America's schoolteachers make less than other comparable professionals in every state. In 2018, they earned 13.1 percent less on average, when accounting for nonwage benefits. So, it's no surprise that teachers, compared to other professions, are roughly 30 percent more likely to work a second job. Despite their low wages, 94 percent of them spend their own money on school supplies for their students. During the 2014–15 school year, they spent, on average, $479 each.[10] That should not happen in a country as wealthy as ours. Our leaders ought to be ashamed. Consider the effect this has on teacher retention. Not surprisingly, 13.8 percent of our nation's teachers leave the profession annually.[11] Factors influencing their decision include:

★ Dissatisfaction with testing and accountability pressures

★ Lack of administrative support

★ Working conditions

★ Money[12]

You probably knew that already. Most of us know teachers, and we've heard all the stories. So, with all that bad PR in circulation, how are we going to attract the most-qualified people to the profession? The number of new teachers is already on the decline. Between 2008 and 2016, there was a 15.4 percent decrease in the number of education degrees awarded and a 27.4 percent drop in the number of people who completed teacher-preparation programs.[13]

Curriculum
If you knew there was a better way to do something, wouldn't you give it a try? We know there are a lot of other countries outperforming us in education, and yet we cling to our old ways.

I suspect it's hubris. Americans like to think we do everything better. Well, we don't. We do a lot of things very well, but we must have the humility to admit when other nations have found a better way. There is so much we can learn from our friends overseas.

Take math, for instance. It's a major reason why students steer away from technology-related fields. A resource center at Stanford University, YouCubed, sums up the state of math education in America:

* Declining interest in math—less than 2 percent of college graduates earn a degree in math

* Severe inequalities for girls and students of color

* Growing need for quantitative literacy in society and employment

* Vast gap between research knowledge and what happens in math classrooms

Through research and workshops, YouCubed has proven that there are better techniques for teaching math, centered not on memorizing formulas and procedures but rather on creativity, critical thinking, and problem-solving.[14] For the most part, however, America's schools are stuck doing the same old thing, with only slight enhancements.

America also needs to provide a pathway for students who are not college bound. For several decades now, Germany has led the way in vocational and technical training. There are plenty of careers that do not require a college degree but do require technical training. Culturally, we've conditioned America's students to believe that college is the only way they can make a good living. We can do a better job providing technical education and presenting it to them as a viable option. Research conducted by Stanford University found that, after California school districts implemented their career-pathway programs, dropout rates in participating districts declined by 23 percent. Politicians have been saying we need to emphasize technical training for decades. It's time they stop talking and just do it.[15]

★

Eleven

THE POLITICS OF DISTRACTION: AMERICA'S ATTENTION DEFICIT DISORDER

I F YOU'VE EVER BEEN TO THE CIRCUS, you may not notice what's happening while you're watching the action. While you're focused on the performance, the next act is being set up in another ring under the cover of darkness. You don't notice because you're fixated on what's happening at that moment. A circus analogy seems quite appropriate when viewing modern politics. A magic analogy works as well. Good magicians know how to draw your attention to one thing while they secretly do something else. As a society, we seem to be easily distracted. Politicians know this and often use one issue as cover to conceal their actual agenda, grabbing onto emotionally charged topics to keep us distracted from what they're really up to.

Donald Trump has used this technique quite effectively, at least with his base. Every day is another attack, another allegation against his enemies, real and perceived. All the while, he uses executive orders to gut environmental regulations, consumer protections, and voter rights. Even when operating out in the open, he manages to promote legislation that working Americans would never support if they fully understood what was really happening. It's a testament to the effectiveness of this strategy that we consistently see people with very little money vote against their own interests.

Let's talk about the most recent tax cut. Working-class Americans were tossed a few dollars, but corporations and the top 1 percent made out like bandits. How is it that people who make so little actually believe the GOP is looking out for them? Over the years, we've become somewhat desensitized to the taxes we pay. Aside from federal, state, real estate, Social Security, and Medicare taxes, we pay sales tax on nearly everything we purchase and every service we use, such as:

* Airplane Tickets

* Fuel

* Cigarettes

* Fishing and Hunting licenses

* Hotel Rooms

* Marriage Licenses

* RVs

* Boats

* Tolls on Bridges and Roads

* Cell Phone Plans

And this is just a short list. We've been conditioned to pay up, almost without question. Sure, we need taxes to support a functioning nation. Taxes allow us to establish regulatory bodies that curb corporate greed and prevent consumer fraud. They support a legal system to protect individual rights and personal safety, at least in theory. I don't know about you, but when I watch most Americans pay their taxes without fail and then watch the wealthy and powerful dodge their responsibilities, I start feeling like I'm being played as a fool.

Let's stop playing their game. Let's rewrite the rules. Let's get wise to the many ways our leaders use distraction to keep our eye off the ball.

Political Distraction in Action

Depending on your age, you may recall when Republicans attacked Bill Clinton for getting a high-priced haircut from a Beverly Hills stylist aboard Air Force One. For his opponents, it was a convenient way to paint him as being out of touch with average Americans. When Ronald Reagan was president, opponents hammered him over wasteful defense expenditures, which included a hammer that cost $435. So much for conservatism and fiscal restraint, right? Government waste is always a handy issue when attempting to throw an incumbent off message.

Sheryl Gay Stolberg wrote about this in the *New York Times*. She says stories used to distract must be simple and should tap into an existing perception or larger concern. Before long, the side issue becomes the main issue. Typically, such storylines create villains and pit good guys against bad guys. "Some distractions are cynical political maneuvers, manufactured by one political party to throw a wrench into the agenda of another," wrote Stolberg. "But the ones that pose the greatest political danger are those that seem to erupt spontaneously, crossing political boundaries, by putting a president at odds with his own party."

As an example, Stolberg points to the massive bailout of insurance company AIG during the Obama administration.

People were outraged when it was revealed the company awarded $165 million in bonuses, despite all the tax dollars used to save it from management's poor stewardship. Stolberg quoted former White House official David Axelrod, who said, "He has a difficult job because he has to explain to the American people, who are furious, why we need to maintain a strong functioning system of credit so that people can get loans and businesses can get loans. At the same time, he has to explain to Wall Street why people are legitimately outraged by what they have done. Both are made more difficult by these kinds of stories."[1]

A Tool to Deflect

Perhaps the most egregious examples of political distraction occur when presidents use the military to change the narrative. It's nearly impossible to prove, but there have certainly been instances when the timing was suspicious. Absent a political insider willing to validate the president's intent, we are left with no smoking gun. For instance, what did Bill Clinton do right after he admitted his affair with Monica Lewinsky? Writing for *The Atlantic*, Dominic Tierney provides an answer and one explanation.

> *"Three days later, with his presidency hanging in the balance, the administration announced airstrikes against suspected terrorist sites in Sudan and Afghanistan, following the bombing of U.S. embassies in Kenya and Tanzania. Many observers claimed that Clinton had launched a classic diversionary war, or a use of force to sidetrack the media, whip up patriotic sentiment, and boost approval ratings."*

Until the election of Donald Trump, such tactics were less overt. As Tierney writes, "Diplomatic moves should be attention-grabbing, symbolic, and popular, particularly among the base. The smartest diversionary actions also have some substantive merit, precisely so the true agenda is harder to spot." Throughout his administration, Trump, however, has not seemed terribly concerned with concealing his true intent. "When negative stories arise, his instinct is to seize the narrative with bold, even outlandish, claims—accusing Barack Obama of wiretapping the phones in Trump Tower, for example," writes Tierney. "If the diversion sets off another firestorm, the solution is further deflection, like a magician whose first trick goes up in smoke and then immediately begins performing a new illusion."[2]

The Complicit Media

Political distraction strategies would not be possible without the media. TV networks, newspapers, and websites all share part of the blame. Most mainstream reporters are accurately reporting the day's events. They're just not looking below the surface. They report what someone says but don't always make the effort to determine if it's true. More to the point, they fail to seek the root causes of a problem or issue. It's not fake news—it's superficial news.

We, as citizens, share part of the blame as well. Media outlets do extensive research to determine what their audience wants. It seems many of us want news that is quick and to the point, if we even want the news at all. We get bored with the same story day after day, so media outlets move on to something else unless there's a compelling reason to advance a story. Their premise is probably accurate. They are giving us what we want. If that were not true, *The PBS News Hour* would have a lot more viewers.

Writing for *The New York Times Magazine*, Mark Leibovich put it quite well:

"Media bosses demand a constant flow of material, which ensures that much reporting remains undigested. Customers want speed or will click elsewhere; competitors spew their own undigested news, and campaigns are only too happy to concoct it, or their opponents will. Shiny objects become tools of our least resistance. Polls and gaffes take less time and brainpower to comprehend than, say, Jeb Bush's book on immigration policy.

"In other words, the press colludes with politicians in this culture of distraction-mongering. Meanwhile, a new class of political figures has built careers almost entirely on shiny-object status. It's more fun than writing policy treatises and much easier than actual governing—and it pays better, too."[3]

★

Twelve

GET IN THE GAME

IN HIS BOOK *Upstream*, DAN HEATH, a Senior Fellow at Duke University's CASE Center, opens with a story about two friends picnicking alongside a river. Soon, a drowning child floats by, and the two rush into the water to save him. No sooner do they make it to shore than another child floats by, and they rush in once again. After several more rescues, one of the friends starts to run up the riverbank, and his friend asks where he's going. He responds that he's going upstream to find out who's throwing all those kids in the river![1]

Upstream is a tremendous book and represents the kind of thinking required to solve some of our country's greatest challenges. Politicians score cheap political points by treating symptoms, like adding more police to fight crime, rather than addressing the root cause of criminal behavior.

This book was never intended to offer specific solutions. Instead it was written to provide perspective on America's problems, who helped create them, and who's making them worse. No one book, no one person could possibly have all the answers. The solutions for each of the problems I've outlined could generate enough books to fill an entire library.

So, what can we do? What can you do? Remember what I wrote at the beginning of this book, in the introduction? I wrote that it's not "normal" to get into politics. That was not written in sarcasm. Moreover, it should be noted that just because someone does not like politics does not mean they don't care. Please allow me to explain what I think it means to be normal:

★ Having no hate in your heart.

★ Respecting all people, regardless of their race, sex, or who they love.

★ Believing the rights outlined in the U.S. Constitution are extended to *all* Americans.

★ You believe everyone should have affordable healthcare.

★ You want every child to receive a quality education.

★ Voting for people who will ensure the care for our disabled veterans.

★ Supporting the crazy idea that every American deserves a living wage and that there are practical ways to lift people out of poverty.

★ Believing that every person and every corporation should pay their fair share in taxes.

★ You detest politics as usual. You want action and practical solutions for the problems that afflict our nation, not partisan lip service and empty promises.

★ You are reluctant to enter the political area, to clash with people who thrive in the swamp, not because you're afraid, but because it's not in your nature to spend precious time away from family and friends, to work among people who don't share your values.

★ You're willing to be a reluctant leader, serve your fellow citizens, and then turn that responsibility over to another reluctant person who will also serve for a brief time—the way the Founders intended.

★ You're nobody's fool.

Please know that nothing will change if we leave it to those who currently lead our nation. They've had plenty of time, and it seems they have little appetite for meaningful reform. However, they do have a big advantage over us, at least for now. They are organized. We are not. They have plenty of resources. We do not. They've twisted voting districts to their advantage and used the courts to legalize the use of limitless dollars to manipulate voters through deceitful means. Yet, we have one powerful tool at our disposal . . . we can still vote.

We must tune out all those manipulative messages and begin to organize. I believe there are two ways forward. We'll consider a long-term solution in the next and final chapter. For the short term, many of you who have been sitting on the sidelines are likely to be political moderates, but you probably lean a little left or a little right. For now, take your sensible attitudes, go to one of the two political parties, and push for moderation. Volunteer. Work your way into party leadership. Vote in primaries. Encourage party members to move closer to the center and farther way from the special interests that have been holding us back. Your country needs you. Sitting this one out will only exacerbate what has become an intolerable imbalance between rich and poor. If you are neither, don't think you're invincible. You're not. One day, you could find yourself at a food bank. I end this chapter once again with the words of the great scholar Clay Jenkinson:

> *"I believe in the dignity of labor, the daycare provider, the nurse in a rural clinic, the welder in a body shop, a retail clerk, or the janitor at a community college. These individuals, born in the same hospitals as the most privileged Americans, swaddled in the same diapers, educated in the same basic curriculum, living under the same constitution, are doing the essential work of our civilization.*
>
> *"I do not believe that the CEO of Starbucks or a broker on Wall Street is better than those people or deserves to live a life of magnificent entitlement and privilege. I do not believe a successful college football coach should earn $5.2 million per year while the philosophy and econ professor earns $70,000. And that is a large salary for most Americans. I understand the market charging what the market will bear. And I believe in economic incentives for success, but I do not believe we are a people that should blithely accept the obscene disparity in American expectations, not just between the rich and the very poor, but between the rich and everybody else."* [2]

★

Thirteen

AN OPEN LETTER TO WARREN BUFFETT

AMERICA IS THE ONLY DEMOCRATIC REPUBLIC in the world that does not have a viable third party. Third parties are invaluable. Even if they do not represent a majority or even a plurality of the voters, they can retain great power, forcing more extreme parties to moderate their positions, producing public policy that serves the largest possible number of people in a manner that is fair to all. A third party is the best option for the long-term preservation of our country. A majority of Americans, 57 percent, say there is a need for a third, major political party, while 38 percent believe the current two-party system does an adequate job of representing the people. These views have been consistent since 2013.[1]

A third party might sound like a pipe dream. It's not, but it would require a lot of work . . . and money. Such a movement begins at the local level and will likely take 10 to 20 years to fully mature. But a third party's influence can be felt much sooner.

All it would take is just a few congressional seats, and, before long, this party—for now, we can call it the American Party or Equality Party—could potentially control 10–15 percent of congress. That's enough to force Republicans and Democrats to do something they have not done in quite some time—compromise. Compromise is more than an act; it's a state of mind. It's the fertile ground that produces public policy that does the most good for the most people.

Setting such a bold plan in motion would require a person of means, someone Republicans could never accuse of being a socialist, a lover of humanity, and someone who values equality and fair play. For me, one name comes to mind: Warren Buffett. So, now, I write directly to you, sir. I admire your commitment to philanthropy and your plan to leave most of your wealth to charity. Given your association with other like-minded billionaires who are doing great things for humanity, I humbly request that you consider making the American (or Equality) Party part of your legacy. You possess not just the financial resources but also the human capital and brainpower to bring together some of our nation's greatest minds to make this a reality.

Every great power in world history has had a beginning and an end. America will likely be no different. Still, we should try to preserve this nation and live up to its highest ideals as long as humanly possible. I am not certain that anything less than a major third party could jolt us from our civic slumber.

★

EPILOGUE

I DIDN'T WRITE THIS BOOK to trash the United States of America. I wrote it to give the frustrated majority a better perspective on the problems we face. If you are among them, I pray that I have convinced you to get involved. Please don't throw up your hands and say, "It's beyond my control." You have more power than you know. Collectively, you, the frustrated majority, are a sleeping giant.

It's easy to retreat from all this, especially if your lives are not all that bad, but you can see the writing on the wall. Many of you know that your lives are not quite as good as they were a few decades—or even a few years—ago. You know your children and grandchildren will have a harder time if something is not done. You belong to a group of mostly decent people. Do you want America to slip further away? Remember, you don't have to do everything—just do *something*.

One final suggestion: I may not be the most persuasive person in the world, and I do not arrogantly believe my words will flip a light switch in everyone's minds. Still, I do have one recommendation. There is some powerful information in this short book. It doesn't take that long to read—maybe a few hours. If all this does not sink in, please read it again. If it still doesn't, read it one more time. The more familiar you become with our nation's situation, the more you will want to act.

If you would like to get involved, please visit www.commonsense2book.com. You can sign up for the mailing list and post your ideas on how we can best address America's most vexing problems.

BIBLIOGRAPHY

Introduction

Huetteman, Emmarie, and Sydney Lupkin. "Drugmakers Funnel Millions to Lawmakers; A Few Dozen Get $100,000-Plus." Kaiser Health News, 23 Aug. 2019, khn.org/news/drugmakers-funnel-millions-to-lawmakers-a-few-dozen-get-100000-plus/.

Chapter 2

"Sweatshops 1880-1940." National Museum of American History, 1 June 2018, americanhistory.si.edu/sweatshops/history-1880-1940.

Sinclair, Upton. *The Jungle*: By Upton Sinclair. Published by Upton Sinclair, 1928.

Joseph Thompson, Mississippi State University. "The GI Bill Should've Been Race Neutral, Politicos Made Sure It Wasn't." *Military Times*, 10 Nov. 2019

Chapter 3

Https://www.washingtonpost.com/Us-Policy/2019/02/27/Top-Tax-Rate-Has-Been-Cut-Six-Times-since-Usually-with-Democrats-Help/.

Vestal, Christine. "New Laws Deepen State Differences Over Abortion." The Pew Charitable Trusts, 30 July 2019, www.pewtrusts.org/en/research-and-analysis/blogs/stateline/2019/07/30/new-laws-deepen-state-differences-over-abortion

Ingraham, Christopher. "There Are More Guns than People in the United States, According to a New Study of Global Firearm Ownership." 19 June 2018.

Bui, Quoctrung. "50 Years of Shrinking Union Membership, in One Map." NPR, 23 Feb. 2015, www.npr.org/sections/money/2015/02/23/385843576/50-years-of-shrinking-union-membership-in-one-map

Crain, Caleb. "State of the Unions: What Happened to America's Labor Movement?" 19 Aug. 2019.

Sherter, Alain. "The U.S. Economy Is 'Broken'—Here's the Proof." *CBS News*, CBS Interactive, 9 Aug. 2017, www.cbsnews.com/news/the-u-s-economy-is-broken-heres-the-proof/

Piketty, Thomas, et al. "Distributional National Accounts: Methods and Estimates for the United States*." *The Quarterly Journal of Economics*, vol. 133, no. 2, 2017, pp. 553–609, doi:10.1093/qje/qjx043

Ross, Martha, and Nicole Bateman. "Low Unemployment Isn't Worth Much If the Jobs Barely Pay." The Brookings Institution, 13 Jan. 2020, www.brookings.edu/blog/the-avenue/2020/01/08/low-unemployment-isnt-worth-much-if-the-jobs-barely-pay/?fbclid=IwAR2YhMTJeF3M9KohOfqSYM-lTbPz5vsDd4l5aA3XHBvBHpJv6721wGIoS2Pc

Gould, Elise. "State of Working America Wages 2019: A Story of Slow, Uneven, and Unequal Wage Growth Over the Last 40 Years." Economic Policy Institute, 20 Feb. 2020, www.epi.org/publication/swa-wages-2019/

Blado, Kayla. "Wage Inequality Continues to Rise as Racial and Gender Disparities Persist: 2019 Data Reveal Slow, Uneven, and Unequal Wage Growth Over the Last 40 Years." Economic Policy Institute, 20 Feb. 2020, www.epi.org/press/wage-inequality-gender-racial-pay-gap/.

Gertner, Leo. "Can't Survive on $7.25: Ten Years Since Last Increase, Congress Still Won't Raise the Minimum Wage." National Employment Law Project, 7 June 2019, www.nelp.org/publication/cant-survive-7-25-ten-years-since-last-increase-congress-still-wont-raise-minimum-wage/

"CPI Inflation Calculator." U.S. Bureau of Labor Statistics, www.bls.gov/data/inflation_calculator.htm

"Median Sales Price of Houses Sold for the United States." FRED, Federal Reserve Bank of St. Louis, 23 Apr. 2020, fred.stlouisfed.org/series/MSPUS

"1980 Buick Regal Limited 2 Door Coupe Prices, Values & Regal Limited 2 Door Coupe Price Specs." NADAguides, National Automobile Dealers Association, www.nadaguides.com/Cars/1980/Buick/Regal-Limited/2-Door-Coupe/Values

"New 2020 Buick Regal Sportback 4dr Sdn Preferred FWD MSRP Prices." NADAguides, National Automobile Dealers Association, www.nadaguides.com/Cars/2020/Buick/Regal-Sportback/4dr-Sdn-Preferred-FWD/Pricing

"Average Undergraduate Tuition and Fees and Room and Board Rates Charged for Full-Time Students in Degree-Granting Institutions, by Type and Control of Institution: 1964-65 through 2006-07." National Center for Education Statistics (NCES) Home Page, a Part of the U.S. Department of Education, nces.ed.gov/programs/digest/d07/tables/dt07_320.asp

"Tuition Costs of Colleges and Universities." National Center for Education Statistics (NCES) Home Page, a Part of the

U.S. Department of Education, nces.ed.gov/fastfacts/display. asp?id=76

"Average Annual Premiums for Single and Family Coverage, 1999-2019." Kaiser Family Foundation, www.kff.org/report-section/ehbs-2019-section-1-cost-of-health-insurance/attachment/figure-1-10-24/

"List Prices Increased as Much as 9 Times Faster Than Inflation for 20 of the Top 25 Part D Drugs, Suggesting Potential for Savings Under Proposed Inflation Rebate Policies." Kaiser Family Foundation, 18 Oct. 2019, www.kff.org/medicare/press-release/list-prices-increased-as-much-as-9-times-faster-than-inflation-for-20-of-the-top-25-part-d-drugs-suggesting-potential-for-savings-under-proposed-inflation-rebate-policies/

"Facts About Hunger and Poverty in America." Feeding America, www.feedingamerica.org/hunger-in-america/facts#:~:text=Facts%20about%20poverty%20and%20hunger%20in%20America&text=More%20than%2054%20million%20people,living%20in%20poverty%20in%20America.&text=More%20than%2037%20million%20people,more%20than%2011%20million%20children

"The Thomas Jefferson Hour." *National Public Radio.* February 5, 2019.

Chapter 4

"Historical Highest Marginal Income Tax Rates." Tax Policy Center, Urban Institute and Brookings Institution, 4 Feb. 2020, www.taxpolicycenter.org/statistics/historical-highest-marginal-income-tax-rates

El-Sibaie, Amir. "2020 Tax Brackets." Tax Foundation, 17 June 2020, taxfoundation.org/2020-tax-brackets/

Ingraham, Christopher. "Analysis: Wealth Concentration Returning to 'Levels Last Seen During the Roaring Twenties,' According to New Research." *The Washington Post*, WP Company, 8 Feb. 2019, www.washingtonpost.com/us-policy/2019/02/08/wealth-concentration-returning-levels-last-seen-during-roaring-twenties-according-new-research/

"Fact Sheet: Corporate Tax Rates." Americans for Tax Fairness, americansfortaxfairness.org/tax-fairness-briefing-booklet/fact-sheet-corporate-tax-rates/

Gardner, Matthew, et al. "Corporate Tax Avoidance Remains Rampant Under New Tax Law." Institution on Taxation and Economic Policy, 11 Apr. 2019, itep.org/notadime/

Chapter 5

Cato Handbook for Policymakers, Cato Institute, 2017.

Mattera, Philip, and Kasia Tarczynska. "Uncle Sam's Favorite Corporations." Good Jobs First, Mar. 2015, www.goodjobsfirst.org/unclesam.

Hohman, James M. "How to Eliminate Corporate Welfare." *The Hill*, 13 Apr. 2019, thehill.com/opinion/finance/438234-how-to-eliminate-corporate-welfare

Slattery, Cailin, and Owen Zidar. "New Data on State and Local Business Tax Incentives Across the U.S." Princeton University, The Trustees of Princeton University, 6 Jan. 2020, economics.princeton.edu/2020/01/06/new-data-on-state-and-local-business-tax-incentives-across-the-u-s/?mod=article_inline

Bort, Julie. "Amazon's New Virginia Data Center Is Getting a Bunch of Tax Breaks, and It Gives Insight into How the Company Reduces Its Tax Liability." *Business Insider*, 19 Feb. 2019, www.businessinsider.com/amazon-data-center-virginia-tax-breaks-2019-2

Mahoney, Laura. "Apple's 22-Year Tax Break Part of Billions in California Bounty (1)." *Bloomberg Industry Group News*, 24 Apr. 2019, news.bloombergtax.com/daily-tax-report-state/apples-22-year-tax-break-part-of-billions-in-california-bounty

The Los Angeles Times Editorial Board. "Editorial: Enough With the Corporate Welfare. California Can Stop the Tax-Break Arms Race." *Los Angeles Times*, 12 Sept. 2019, www.latimes.com/opinion/story/2019-09-11/no-tax-sharing-bill-amazon-california

Shukovsky, Paul. "Boeing's $8.7 Billion Washington State Tax Break Under Scrutiny (1)." *Bloomberg Industry Group News*, 9 Oct. 2019, news.bloombergtax.com/daily-tax-report-state/boeings-8-7-billion-washington-state-tax-break-under-scrutiny

Constant, Paul. "It's Time to End Corporate Welfare. Boeing Is Exhibit A for Why." *Business Insider*, 23 Jan. 2020, www.businessinsider.com/its-time-to-end-corporate-welfare-boeing-is-exhibit-a-2020-1

Chapter 6

"Americans Still Hold Dim View of U.S. Healthcare System." Gallup.com, 11 Dec. 2017, news.gallup.com/poll/223403/americans-hold-dim-view-healthcare-system.aspx

Feldscher, Karen. "U.S. Pays More for Health Care with Worse Population Health Outcomes." *Harvard Gazette*, 13 Mar. 2018, news.harvard.edu/gazette/story/2018/03/u-s-pays-more-for-health-care-with-worse-population-health-outcomes/

Loudenback, Tanza. "The Average Cost of Healthcare in 21 Different Countries." *Business Insider*, 7 Mar. 2019, www.businessinsider.com/personal-finance/cost-of-healthcare-countries-ranked-2019-3

Papanicolas, Irene, et al. "Health Care Spending in the United States and Other High-Income Countries." *JAMA*, U.S. National Library of Medicine, 13 Mar. 2018, pubmed.ncbi. nlm.nih.gov/29536101/

Kane, Jason. "Health Costs: How the U.S. Compares With Other Countries." Public Broadcasting Service, 22 Oct. 2012, www.pbs.org/newshour/health/health-costs-how-the-us -compares-with-other-countries

Langreth, Robert. "Drug Prices." Bloomberg.com, 5 Feb. 2019, www.bloomberg.com/quicktake/drug-prices

United States Congress House Ways and Means Committee. *A Painful Pill to Swallow: U.S. vs. International Prescription Drug Prices.* Government Printing Office, 2019.

Blumberg, Yoni. "Here's Why Many Prescription Drugs in the US Cost so Much—and It's Not Innovation or Improvement." CNBC, 14 Jan. 2019, www.cnbc.com/2019/01/10/why-pre-scription-drugs-in-the-us-cost-so-much.html

Ekaterina Galkina Cleary, Jennifer M. Beierlein, Navleen Surjit Khanuja, Laura M. McNamee, and Fred D. Ledley, "Contribution of NIH funding to new drug approvals 2010–2016," *Proceedings of the National Academy of Sciences of the United States of America*, Mar. 2018, 115 (10) 2329-2334; DOI: 10.1073/pnas.1715368115

Cone, Jason. "Pharmaceutical Corporations Need to Stop Free-Riding on Publicly Funded Research." *The Hill*, Capitol Hill Publishing Corp., 3 Mar. 2018, thehill.com/ opinion/healthcare/376574-pharmaceutical-corpora-tions-need-to-stop-free-riding-on-publicly-funded

Langreth, Robert, et al. "The U.S. Pays a Lot More for Top Drugs Than Other Countries." Bloomberg.com, 18 Dec. 2015, www.bloomberg.com/graphics/2015-drug-prices/

"Fact Sheet: Uncompensated Hospital Care Cost: AHA." American Hospital Association, Jan. 2020, www.aha.org/ fact-sheets/2020-01-06-fact-sheet-uncompensated-hospital-care-cost

"FAQs." Physicians for a National Health Program, 5 Aug. 2019, pnhp.org/what-is-single-payer/faqs/

"Medical Debt, Medical Bankruptcy and the Impact on Patients." National Patient Advocate Foundation, National Patient Advocate Foundation, Aug. 2014, www.npaf.org/wp-content/ uploads/2017/07/Medical-Debt-White-Paper.pdf

Chapter 7

America's Wars, Department of Veterans Affairs, Nov. 2019, www.va.gov/opa/publications/factsheets/fs_americas_wars.pdf

Toft, Monica Duffy. "Why Is America Addicted to Foreign Interventions?" *The National Interest*, The Center for the National Interest, 11 June 2018, nationalinterest.org/feature/ why-america-addicted-foreign-interventions-23582

"U.S. Defense Spending Compared to Other Countries." Peter G. Peterson Foundation, 13 May 2020, www.pgpf.org/ chart-archive/0053_defense-comparison

Eisenhower, Dwight D. "Military-Industrial Complex Speech, Dwight D. Eisenhower, 1961." *Avalon Project—Military-Industrial Complex Speech, Dwight D. Eisenhower, 1961*, Yale Law School Lillian Goldman Law Library, 1961, avalon.law. yale.edu/20th_century/eisenhower001.asp

U.S. Department of Defense, Office of the Under Secretary of Defense for Acquisition and Sustainment. "Report to Congress Section 889 of the FY 2018 NDAA Report on Defense Contracting Fraud." December 2018, https://fas. org/man/eprint/contract-fraud.pdf

"These Atomic Bomb Tests Used U.S. Troops as Guinea Pigs."
Smithsonian.com, Smithsonian Institution, www.smithso-
nianmag.com/videos/category/history/these-atomic-bomb-tests
-used-us-troops-as/

Dickerson, Caitlin. "Secret World War II Chemical Experiments
Tested Troops by Race." *National Public Radio*, 22 June 2015,
www.npr.org/2015/06/22/415194765/u-s-troops-tested-by-
race-in-secret-world-war-ii-chemical-experiments

Centers for Disease Control and Prevention, 4 Apr. 2018, emer-
gency.cdc.gov/agent/sulfurmustard/basics/facts.asp

Hixenbaugh, Mike, and Charles Ornstein. "For Decades, the VA
Turned to 1 Man on Whether Agent Orange Harmed Vets.
His Reliable Answer: No." Pilotonline.com, *The Virginian-
Pilot*, 26 Oct. 2016, www.pilotonline.com/military/arti-
cle_f6b15a6f-acc6-5360-9a38-f6e6d31021c1.html

Hixenbaugh, Mike, and Charles Ornstein. "When VA Is Deciding
on Agent Orange Benefits, Science Sometimes Takes Backseat
to Politics and Cost." Pilotonline.com, *The Virginian-Pilot*, 15
June 2016, www.pilotonline.com/military/article_db7bacae-
3e67-564c-95ad-e10c4238cba9.html

Ornstein, Charles, and Mike Hixenbaugh. "Agent Orange Curse:
Vietnam Vets Can Pass Birth Defects to Their Kids, New
Data Suggests." Pilotonline.com, *The Virginian-Pilot*, 16 Dec.
2016, www.pilotonline.com/military/article_1c284628-2dbe-
510d-98a2-40b639759943.html

Zundel, Clara G., et al. "Rates of Chronic Medical Conditions in
1991 Gulf War Veterans Compared to the General Population."
MDPI, Multidisciplinary Digital Publishing Institute, 16 Mar.
2019, www.mdpi.com/1660-4601/16/6/949/htm

Kime, Patricia. "VA Gets 'F' for Persian Gulf War Claims Approvals."
Military Times, 15 Mar. 2016, www.militarytimes.com

/veterans/2016/03/15/va-gets-f-for-persian-gulf-war-claims-approvals/

Urbi, Jaden. "The VA's History of Setbacks and Missteps." *CNBC*, 28 May 2018, www.cnbc.com/2018/05/28/va-veterans-affairs-history-setbacks-missteps.html

Chapter 8

King, Dr. Martin Luther. "Letter from a Birmingham Jail." African Studies Center-University of Pennsylvania, 16 Apr. 1963, www.africa.upenn.edu/Articles_Gen/Letter_Birmingham.html

Edwards, Frank, et al. "Risk of Being Killed by Police Use of Force in the United States by Age, Race-Ethnicity, and Sex." National Academy of Sciences, 20 Aug. 2019, www.pnas.org/content/116/34/16793

Staff, ACLU. "The War on Marijuana in Black and White." American Civil Liberties Union, 22 Oct. 2018, www.aclu.org/issues/smart-justice/sentencing-reform/war-marijuana-black-and-white

"Race and the Drug War." Drug Policy Alliance, www.drugpolicy.org/issues/race-and-drug-war

"11 Facts About Racial Discrimination." DoSomething.org, www.dosomething.org/us/facts/11-facts-about-racial-discrimination

"What Is Systemic Racism? [VIDEOS]." Race Forward, 4 June 2020, www.raceforward.org/videos/systemic-racism

Walker, Jonathan D. "Health Care System a Major Factor in African Americans' Poorer Health." Physicians for a National Health Program, June 2012, pnhp.org/news/health-care-system-a-major-factor-in-african-americans-poorer-health/

"Racial Economic Inequality." Inequality.org, inequality.org/facts/racial-inequality/

Bruenig, Matt. "The Top 10 Percent of White Families Own Almost Everything." *The American Prospect*, Demos, 8 Sept. 2014, prospect.org/power/top-10-percent-white-families -almost-everything/

"23 Billion." EdBuild, Mar. 2019, edbuild.org/content/23-billion

Lutton, Linda, et al. "Home Loans in Chicago: One Dollar to White Neighborhoods, 12 Cents to Black." "Home Mortgage Lending Inequality in Chicago," WBEZ, 3 June 2020, inter-active.wbez.org/2020/banking/disparity/

"2016 Hate Crime Statistics." Federal Bureau of Investigation, 13 Nov. 2017, www.fbi.gov/news/stories/2016-hate-crime-statistics

"2018 Hate Crime Statistics Released." Federal Bureau of Investigation, 12 Nov. 2019, www.fbi.gov/news/ stories/2018-hate-crime-statistics-released-111219

Taylor, Ryan. "Kimberly Latrice Jones BLM Video Speech Transcript." *Rev*, 8 June 2020, www.rev.com/blog/transcripts/ kimberly-latrice-jones-blm-video-speech-transcript

Chapter 9

Millhiser, Ian. "Never Count on the Supreme Court to Protect Voting Rights." *The New Republic*, 22 Mar. 2015, newre-public.com/article/121323/supreme-courts-history-voting -rights-injustices-excerpt

"Reconstruction in America: EJI Report." EJI Reports, 7 July 2020, eji.org/report/reconstruction-in-america/

"Voting Irregularities in Florida During the 2000 Presidential Election." Executive Summary, United States Civil Rights Commission, June 2001, www.usccr.gov/pubs/vote2000/ report/exesum.htm

"Missouri, 2000." Brennan Center for Justice, 10 Nov. 2007, www. brennancenter.org/our-work/research-reports/missouri-2000

"*Shelby County v. Holder.*" Brennan Center for Justice, 4 Aug. 2018, www.brennancenter.org/our-work/court-cases/shelby-county-v-holder

Caputo, Angela, et al. "How a Massive Voter Purge in Georgia Affected the 2018 Election." *APM Reports*, 29 Oct. 2019, www.apmreports.org/story/2019/10/29/georgia-voting-registration-records-removed

Judd, Alan. "Georgia's Strict Laws Lead to Large Purge of Voters." *The Atlanta Journal-Constitution*, 30 Oct. 2018, www.ajc.com/news/state--regional-govt--politics/voter-purge-begs-question-what-the-matter-with-georgia/YAFvuk3Bu95kJIMaDiDFqJ/.

Rouan, Rick. "Vast Majority of the 180,000 Ohio Voters Purged Because They Didn't Vote." *The Columbus Dispatch*, 39 Sept. 2019, www.dispatch.com/news/20190930/vast-majority-of-180000-ohio-voters-purged-because-they-didnt-vote

Ingraham, Christopher. "Analysis: This Anti-Voter-Fraud Program Gets It Wrong Over 99 Percent of the Time. The GOP Wants to Take It Nationwide." *The Washington Post*, WP Company, 20 July 2017, www.washingtonpost.com/news/wonk/wp/2017/07/20/this-anti-voter-fraud-program-gets-it-wrong-over-99-of-the-time-the-gop-wants-to-take-it-nationwide/

Levitt, Justin. "A Comprehensive Investigation of Voter Impersonation Finds 31 Credible Incidents out of One Billion Ballots Cast." *The Washington Post*, WP Company, 6 Aug. 2014, www.washingtonpost.com/news/wonk/wp/2014/08/06/a-comprehensive-investigation-of-voter-impersonation-finds-31-credible-incidents-out-of-one-billion-ballots-cast/

Anderson, Carol. *One Person, No Vote: How Voter Suppression Is Destroying Our Democracy.* Bloomsbury Publishing, 2019.

"Public Housing ID Not Valid Voter Photo ID in Alabama."
NAACP Legal Defense and Educational Fund, 4 Nov. 2014,
www.naacpldf.org/press-release/public-housing-id-not-valid
-voter-photo-id-in-alabama/

Reilly, Ryan J. "Judges Seem Ready to Mess With Texas' Voter
ID Law." Talking Points Memo, 13 July 2012, talking-
pointsmemo.com/muckraker/judges-seem-ready-to-mess
-with-texas-voter-id-law

Johnson, Theodore R., and Max Feldman. "The New Voter
Suppression." Brennan Center for Justice, 16 Jan. 2020,
www.brennancenter.org/our-work/research-reports/
new-voter-suppression

Maxwell, Connor, and Danielle Root. "Five Truths About
Voter Suppression." Center for American Progress,
12 Mar. 2017, www.americanprogress.org/issues/race/
news/2017/05/12/432339/five-truths-voter-suppression/

"Voter ID." Georgia Department of Driver Services, dds.georgia.
gov/voter-id

Horwitz, Sari. "Getting a Photo ID so You Can Vote Is Easy.
Unless You're Poor, Black, Latino or Elderly." *The Washington
Post*, WP Company, 23 May 2016, www.washingtonpost.
com/politics/courts_law/getting-a-photo-id-so-you-can-vote-
is-easy-unless-youre-poor-black-latino-or-elderly/2016/05/23/
8d5474ec-20f0-11e6-8690-f14ca9de2972_story.html

Voter Registration Statistics, North Carolina State Board
of Elections, 13 June 2020, vt.ncsbe.gov/RegStat/
Results/?date=06%2F13%2F2020

Daley, David. "The Secret Files of the Master of Modern
Republican Gerrymandering." *The New Yorker*, 6 Sept.
2019, www.newyorker.com/news/news-desk/the-se-
cret-files-of-the-master-of-modern-republican-gerrymandering

"Democrats Cry Foul as House Republicans Redraw District Lines." *The Atlanta Journal-Constitution*, 9 Mar. 2017, www.ajc.com/news/state--regional-govt--politics/democrats-cry-foul-house-republicans-redraw-district-lines/sOOXVi3vMCWJCB7gpAntTN/

Berman, Ari. "Texas' Redistricting Maps and Voter-ID Law Intentionally Discriminated Against Minority Voters." *The Nation*, 13 Mar. 2017, www.thenation.com/article/archive/texass-redistricting-maps-and-voter-id-law-intentionally-discriminated-against-minority-voters/

Wolf, Thomas. "Bringing Whitford Into Focus. What You Should Know about One of the Most Pivotal Cases in Decades on How Congressional Maps Are Drawn," Brennan Center for Justice, 8 Aug. 2017, www.brennancenter.org/our-work/analysis-opinion/bringing-whitford-focus

Daley, David. "Meet the Man Who May End Gerrymandering: A Retired Wisconsin Law Professor's Supreme Court Case Could Save Democracy." *Salon*, Salon.com, 26 Mar. 2017, www.salon.com/2017/03/26/meet-the-man-who-may-end-gerrymandering-a-retired-wisconsin-law-professors-supreme-court-case-could-save-democracy/

Lau, Tim. "*Citizens United* Explained." Brennan Center for Justice, 12 Dec. 2019, www.brennancenter.org/our-work/research-reports/citizens-united-explained

Chapter 10

Sargrad, Scott, et al. "A Quality Education for Every Child." Center for American Progress, 2 June 2019, www.americanprogress.org/issues/education-k-12/reports/2019/07/02/471511/quality-education-every-child/

Jacob, Brian A. "How the U.S. Department of Education Can Foster Education Reform in the Era of Trump and ESSA." The Brookings Institution, 2 Feb. 2017, www.brookings.edu/research/how-the-u-s-department-of-education-can-foster-education-reform-in-the-era-of-trump-and-essa/

"K-12 Facts." The Center for Education Reform, 19 Dec. 2019, edreform.com/2012/04/k-12-facts/#Snapshot

DeSilver, Drew. "U.S. Academic Achievement Lags That of Many Other Countries." Pew Research Center, 15 Feb. 2017, www.pewresearch.org/fact-tank/2017/02/15/u-s-students-internationally-math-science/

"The NCES Fast Facts Tool Provides Quick Answers to Many Education Questions (National Center for Education Statistics)." National Center for Education Statistics (NCES) Home Page, a Part of the U.S. Department of Education, 2016, nces.ed.gov/fastfacts/display.asp?id=1

"The State of America's Children 2020—Child Poverty." Children's Defense Fund, Feb. 2020, www.childrensdefense.org/policy/resources/soac-2020-child-poverty/

McGuire, Kent. "Time to Put Poverty Back on the Education Reform Agenda." *Philanthropy News Digest* Candid, 19 May 2014, philanthropynewsdigest.org/commentary-and-opinion/time-to-put-poverty-back-on-the-education-reform-agenda

"K-12 Disparity Facts and Statistics." United Negro College Fund, uncf.org/pages/k-12-disparity-facts-and-stats

Jackson, C. K., Johnson, R. C., & Persico, C. (2016). "The effects of school spending on educational and economic outcomes: Evidence from school finance reforms." *Quarterly Journal of Economics,* 131(1), 157-218. [qjv036]. https://doi.org/10.1093/qje/qjv036

Carver-Thomas, Desiree, and Linda Darling-Hammond. "Teacher Turnover: Why It Matters and What We Can Do About It." Learning Policy Institute, Aug. 2017, learningpolicyinstitute.org/sites/default/files/product-files/Teacher_Turnover_REPORT.pdf

Garcia, Emma, and Elaine Weiss. "U.S. Schools Struggle to Hire and Retain Teachers: The Second Report in 'The Perfect Storm in the Teacher Labor Market' Series." Economic Policy Institute, 16 Apr. 2019, www.epi.org/publication/u-s-schools-struggle-to-hire-and-retain-teachers-the-second-report-in-the-perfect-storm-in-the-teacher-labor-market-series/

"Our Mission." YouCubed, www.youcubed.org/our-mission/

Spector, Carrie. "Schools That Received State Funds to Expand Career Training Programs Saw Lower Dropout Rates, Stanford Researcher Finds." Stanford Graduate School of Education, Stanford University, 15 May 2019, ed.stanford.edu/news/schools-received-state-funds-expand-career-training-programs-saw-lower-dropout-rates-stanford#:~:text=A%20new%20study%20by%20a,a%20doctoral%20candidate%20at%20Stanford

Chapter 11

Stolberg, Sheryl Gay. "The Art of Political Distraction." *The New York Times*, 21 Mar. 2009, www.nytimes.com/2009/03/22/weekinreview/22stolberg.html?mtrref=www.google.com&gwh=F900AD35B3B4CE3210542D852DB-3D015&gwt=%E2%80%A6

Tierney, Dominic. "The Risks of Foreign Policy as Political Distraction." *The Atlantic*, Atlantic Media Company, 15 June 2017, www.theatlantic.com/international/archive/2017/06/trump-diversionary-foreign-policy/530079/

Leibovich, Mark. "The Politics of Distraction." *The New York Times*, 1 Sept. 2015, www.nytimes.com/2015/09/06/magazine/the-politics-of-distraction.html?auth=linked-google

Chapter 12
Heath, Dan. *Upstream: The Quest to Solve Problems before They Happen.* Avid Reader Press, 2020.

Chapter 13
Reinhart, RJ. "Majority in U.S. Still Say a Third Party Is Needed." Gallup.com, 26 Oct. 2018, news.gallup.com/poll/244094/majority-say-third-party-needed.aspx

ENDNOTES

Introduction

1. Huetteman, Emmarie, and Sydney Lupkin. "Drugmakers Funnel Millions to Lawmakers; A Few Dozen Get $100,000-Plus." Kaiser Health News, 23 Aug. 2019, khn.org/news/drugmakers-funnel-millions-to-lawmakers-a-few-dozen-get-100000-plus/.

Chapter Two

1. "Sweatshops 1880-1940." National Museum of American History, 1 June 2018, americanhistory.si.edu/sweatshops/history-1880-1940.

2. Sinclair, Upton. *The Jungle*: By Upton Sinclair. Published by Upton Sinclair, 1928.

3. "Sweatshops 1880-1940." National Museum of American History, 1 June 2018, americanhistory.si.edu/sweatshops/history-1880-1940.

4. Joseph Thompson, Mississippi State University. "The GI Bill Should've Been Race Neutral, Politicos Made Sure It Wasn't." *Military Times*, 10 Nov. 2019, www.militarytimes.

com/military-honor/salute-veterans/2019/11/10/the-gi-bill-
shouldve-been-race-neutral-politicos-made-sure-it-wasnt/

Chapter Three

1. Ingraham, Christopher. "The Top Tax Rate Has Been Cut Six Times since 1980—Usually with Democrats' Help." *The Washington Post*, 27 Feb. 2019.

2. Vestal, Christine. "New Laws Deepen State Differences Over Abortion." The Pew Charitable Trusts, 30 July 2019, www.pewtrusts.org/en/research-and-analysis/blogs/stateline/2019/07/30/new-laws-deepen-state-differences-over-abortion

3. Ingraham, Christopher. "There Are More Guns than People in the United States, According to a New Study of Global Firearm Ownership." 19 June 2018

4. Bui, Quoctrung. "50 Years of Shrinking Union Membership, in One Map." NPR, 23 Feb. 2015, www.npr.org/sections/money/2015/02/23/385843576/50-years-of-shrinking-union-membership-in-one-map

5. Crain, Caleb. "State of the Unions: What Happened to America's Labor Movement?" 19 Aug. 2019.

6. Sherter, Alain. "The U.S. Economy Is 'Broken'—Here's the Proof." *CBS News*, CBS Interactive, 9 Aug. 2017, www.cbsnews.com/news/the-u-s-economy-is-broken-heres-the-proof/

7. Piketty, Thomas, et al. "Distributional National Accounts: Methods and Estimates for the United States*." *The Quarterly Journal of Economics*, vol. 133, no. 2, 2017, pp. 553–609., doi:10.1093/qje/qjx043.

8. Ross, Martha, and Nicole Bateman. "Low Unemployment Isn't Worth Much If the Jobs Barely Pay." The Brookings Institution, 13 Jan. 2020, www.brookings.edu/blog/

the-avenue/2020/01/08/low-unemployment-isnt-worth
-much-if-the-jobs-barely-pay/?fbclid=IwAR2YhMT-
JeF3M9KohOfqSYMlTbPz5vsDd4l5aA3XHBvBHp-
Jv6721wGIoS2Pc

9. Gould, Elise. "State of Working America Wages 2019: A
    Story of Slow, Uneven, and Unequal Wage Growth Over
    the Last 40 Years." Economic Policy Institute, 20 Feb. 2020,
    www.epi.org/publication/swa-wages-2019/

10. Blado, Kayla. "Wage Inequality Continues to Rise as
    Racial and Gender Disparities Persist: 2019 Data
    Reveal Slow, Uneven, and Unequal Wage Growth
    Over the Last 40 Years." Economic Policy Institute, 20
    Feb. 2020, www.epi.org/press/wage-inequality-gender
    -racial-pay-gap/

11. Gould, Elise. "State of Working America Wages 2019: A
    Story of Slow, Uneven, and Unequal Wage Growth Over
    the Last 40 Years." Economic Policy Institute, 20 Feb. 2020,
    www.epi.org/publication/swa-wages-2019/

12. Gertner, Leo. "Can't Survive on $7.25: Ten Years Since Last
    Increase, Congress Still Won't Raise the Minimum Wage."
    National Employment Law Project, 7 June 2019, www.
    nelp.org/publication/cant-survive-7-25-ten-years-since-last-
    increase-congress-still-wont-raise-minimum-wage/

13. U.S. Bureau of Labor Statistics Consumer Price Index
    Calculator

14. "Median Sales Price of Houses Sold for the United States."
    Economic Research-Federal Reserve Bank of St. Louis, https://
    fred.stlouisfed.org/series/MSPUS

15. "1980 Buick Regal Limited Prices and Values." *NADA
    Guides*, https://www.nadaguides.com/Cars/1980/Buick/
    Regal-Limited/2-Door-Coupe/Values

16. "2020 Buick Regal Sportback Base Price." *NADA Guides.* https://www.nadaguides.com/Cars/2020/Buick/Regal-Sportback/4dr-Sdn-Preferred-FWD/Pricing

17. "Average undergraduate tuition and fees and room and board rates charged for full-time students in degree-granting institutions, by type and control of institution: 1964-65 through 2006-07." National Center for Education Statistics, https://nces.ed.gov/programs/digest/d07/tables/dt07_320.asp

18. "Tuition costs of colleges and universities." National Center for Education Statistics, https://nces.ed.gov/fastfacts/display.asp?id=76

19. "Average Annual Premiums for Single and Family Coverage, 1999-2019." Kaiser Family Foundation, https://www.kff.org/report-section/ehbs-2019-section-1-cost-of-health-insurance/attachment/figure-1-10-24/

20. "List Prices Increased as Much as 9 Times Faster Than Inflation for 20 of the Top 25 Part D Drugs, Suggesting Potential for Savings Under Proposed Inflation Rebate Policies." Kaiser Family Foundation, October 18, 2019, https://www.kff.org/medicare/press-release/list-prices-increased-as-much-as-9-times-faster-than-inflation-for-20-of-the-top-25-part-d-drugs-suggesting-potential-for-savings-under-proposed-inflation-rebate-policies/

21. "Facts about poverty and hunger in America." Feeding America, https://www.feedingamerica.org/hunger-in-america/facts#:~:text=Facts%20about%20poverty%20and%20hunger%20in%20America&text=More%20than%2054%20million%20people,living%20in%20poverty%20in%20America.&text=More%20than%2037%20million%20people,more%20than%2011%20million%20children

22. "The Thomas Jefferson Hour." *National Public Radio.* February 5, 2019.

Chapter Four

1. "Historical Highest Marginal Income Tax Rates 1913 to 2020." Tax Policy Center, https://www.taxpolicycenter.org/statistics/historical-highest-marginal-income-tax-rates

2. El-Sibaie, Amir. "2020 Tax Brackets." Tax Foundation, 17 June 2020, taxfoundation.org/2020-tax-brackets/

3. Ingraham, Christopher. "Analysis: Wealth Concentration Returning to 'Levels Last Seen During the Roaring Twenties,' According to New Research." *The Washington Post*, WP Company, 8 Feb. 2019, www.washingtonpost.com/us-policy/2019/02/08/wealth-concentration-returning-levels-last-seen-during-roaring-twenties-according-new-research/.

4. Ingraham, Christopher. "Analysis: Wealth Concentration Returning to 'Levels Last Seen During the Roaring Twenties,' According to New Research." *The Washington Post*, WP Company, 8 Feb. 2019, www.washingtonpost.com/us-policy/2019/02/08/wealth-concentration-returning-levels-last-seen-during-roaring-twenties-according-new-research/

5. Ingraham, Christopher. "Analysis: Wealth Concentration Returning to 'Levels Last Seen During the Roaring Twenties,' According to New Research." *The Washington Post*, WP Company, 8 Feb. 2019, www.washingtonpost.com/us-policy/2019/02/08/wealth-concentration-returning-levels-last-seen-during-roaring-twenties-according-new-research/

6. Ingraham, Christopher. "Analysis: Wealth Concentration Returning to 'Levels Last Seen During the Roaring Twenties,' According to New Research." *The Washington*

Post, WP Company, 8 Feb. 2019, www.washingtonpost.com/us-policy/2019/02/08/wealth-concentration-returning-levels-last-seen-during-roaring-twenties-according-new-research/

7. "Fact Sheet: Corporate Tax Rates." Americans for Tax Fairness, https://americansfortaxfairness.org/tax-fairness-briefing-booklet/fact-sheet-corporate-tax-rates/

8. Gardner, Matthew, et al. "Corporate Tax Avoidance Remains Rampant Under New Tax Law." Institution on Taxation and Economic Policy, 11 Apr. 2019, itep.org/notadime/

Chapter Five

1. Cato Institute, *Cato Handbook for Policymakers*, Cato Institute, 2017

2. Mattera, Philip, and Kasia Tarczynska. "Uncle Sam's Favorite Corporations." Good Jobs First, Mar. 2015, www.goodjobsfirst.org/unclesam

3. Hohman, James M. "How to Eliminate Corporate Welfare." *The Hill*, 13 Apr. 2019, thehill.com/opinion/finance/438234-how-to-eliminate-corporate-welfare

4. Slattery, Cailin, and Owen Zidar. "New Data on State and Local Business Tax Incentives across the U.S." Princeton University, The Trustees of Princeton University, 6 Jan. 2020, economics.princeton.edu/2020/01/06/new-data-on-state-and-local-business-tax-incentives-across-the-u-s/?mod=article_inline

5. Bort, Julie. "Amazon's New Virginia Data Center Is Getting a Bunch of Tax Breaks, and It Gives Insight Into How the Company Reduces Its Tax Liability." *Business Insider*, 19 Feb. 2019, www.businessinsider.com/amazon-data-center-virginia-tax-breaks-2019-2.

6. Slattery, Cailin, and Owen Zidar. "New Data on State and Local Business Tax Incentives Across the U.S." Princeton University, The Trustees of Princeton University, 6 Jan. 2020, economics.princeton.edu/2020/01/06/new-data-on-state-and-local-business-tax-incentives-across-the-u-s/?mod=article_inline

7. Mahoney, Laura. "Apple's 22-Year Tax Break Part of Billions in California Bounty (1)." *Bloomberg Industry Group News*, 24 Apr. 2019, news.bloombergtax.com/daily-tax-report-state/apples-22-year-tax-break-part-of-billions-in-california-bounty

8. The Times Editorial Board. "Editorial: Enough with the corporate welfare. California can stop the tax-break arms race." *Los Angeles Times*, 21 Sept. 2019, https://www.latimes.com/opinion/story/2019-09-11/no-tax-sharing-bill-amazon-california

9. Shukovsky, Paul. "Boeing's $8.7 Billion Washington State Tax Break Under Scrutiny (1)." *Bloomberg Industry Group News*, 9 Oct. 2019, news.bloombergtax.com/daily-tax-report-state/boeings-8-7-billion-washington-state-tax-break-under-scrutiny

10. Constant, Paul. "It's Time to End Corporate Welfare. Boeing Is Exhibit A for Why." *Business Insider*, 23 Jan. 2020, www.businessinsider.com/its-time-to-end-corporate-welfare-boeing-is-exhibit-a-2020-

Chapter Six

1. "Americans Still Hold Dim View of U.S. Healthcare System." Gallup.com, Gallup, 11 Dec. 2017, news.gallup.com/poll/223403/americans-hold-dim-view-healthcare-system.aspx

2. Feldscher, Karen. "U.S. Pays More for Health Care with Worse Population Health Outcomes." *Harvard Gazette*, 13 Mar. 2018, news.harvard.edu/gazette/story/2018/03/u-s-pays-more-for-health-care-with-worse-population-health-outcomes/

3. Loudenback, Tanza. "The Average Cost of Healthcare in 21 Different Countries." *Business Insider*, 7 Mar. 2019, www.businessinsider.com/personal-finance/cost-of-healthcare-countries-ranked-2019-3

4. Papanicolas, Irene, et al. "Health Care Spending in the United States and Other High-Income Countries," *JAMA*, U.S. National Library of Medicine, 13 Mar. 2018, pubmed.ncbi.nlm.nih.gov/29536101/

5. Papanicolas, Irene, et al. "Health Care Spending in the United States and Other High-Income Countries." *JAMA*, U.S. National Library of Medicine, 13 Mar. 2018, pubmed.ncbi.nlm.nih.gov/29536101/

6. Kane, Jason. "Health Costs: How the U.S. Compares With Other Countries." *Public Broadcasting Service*, 22 Oct. 2012, www.pbs.org/newshour/health/health-costs-how-the-us-compares-with-other-countries

7. Kane, Jason. "Health Costs: How the U.S. Compares With Other Countries." *Public Broadcasting Service*, 22 Oct. 2012, www.pbs.org/newshour/health/health-costs-how-the-us-compares-with-other-countries

8. Kane, Jason. "Health Costs: How the U.S. Compares With Other Countries." *Public Broadcasting Service*, 22 Oct. 2012, www.pbs.org/newshour/health/health-costs-how-the-us-compares-with-other-countries

9. Langreth, Robert. "Drug Prices." Bloomberg.com, Bloomberg, 5 Feb. 2019, www.bloomberg.com/quicktake/drug-prices

10. United States Congress, House Ways and Means Committee. *A Painful Pill to Swallow: U.S. vs. International Prescription Drug Prices.* Government Printing Office, 2019

11. Blumberg, Yoni. "Here's Why Many Prescription Drugs in the US Cost so Much—and It's Not Innovation or Improvement." *CNBC*, 14 Jan. 2019, www.cnbc.com/2019/01/10/why-prescription-drugs-in-the-us-cost-so-much.html

12. Ekaterina Galkina Cleary, Jennifer M. Beierlein, Navleen Surjit Khanuja, Laura M. McNamee, and Fred D. Ledley, "Contribution of NIH funding to new drug approvals 2010–2016," *Proceedings of the National Academy of Sciences of the United States of America*, Mar. 2018, 115 (10) 2329-2334; DOI: 10.1073/pnas.1715368115

13. Cone, Jason. "Pharmaceutical Corporations Need to Stop Free-Riding on Publicly Funded Research." *The Hill*, Capitol Hill Publishing Corp., 3 Mar. 2018, thehill.com/opinion/healthcare/376574-pharmaceutical-corporations-need-to-stop-free-riding-on-publicly-funded

14. Langreth, Robert, et al. "The U.S. Pays a Lot More for Top Drugs Than Other Countries." Bloomberg.com, Bloomberg, 18 Dec. 2015, www.bloomberg.com/graphics/2015-drug-prices/

15. United States Congress, House Ways and Means Committee, *A Painful Pill to Swallow: U.S. vs. International Prescription Drug Prices* Government Printing Office, 2019

16. "Fact Sheet: Uncompensated Hospital Care Cost." American Hospital Association, Jan. 2020, www.aha.org/fact-sheets/2020-01-06-fact-sheet-uncompensated-hospital-care-cost

17. "FAQs." Physicians for a National Health Program, 5 Aug. 2019, pnhp.org/what-is-single-payer/faqs/

18. "Medical Debt, Medical Bankruptcy and the Impact on Patients." National Patient Advocate Foundation, National Patient Advocate Foundation, Aug. 2014, www.npaf.org/wp-content/uploads/2017/07/Medical-Debt-White-Paper.pdf.

Chapter Seven

1. *America's Wars*, Department of Veterans Affairs, Nov. 2019, www.va.gov/opa/publications/factsheets/fs_americas_wars.pdf

2. Toft, Monica Duffy. "Why Is America Addicted to Foreign Interventions?" The National Interest, The Center for the National Interest, 11 June 2018, nationalinterest.org/feature/why-america-addicted-foreign-interventions-23582

3. "U.S. Defense Spending Compared to Other Countries." Peter G. Peterson Foundation, 13 May 2020, www.pgpf.org/chart-archive/0053_defense-comparison.

4. Eisenhower, Dwight D. "Military-Industrial Complex Speech, Dwight D. Eisenhower, 1961." *Avalon Project—Military-Industrial Complex Speech*, Dwight D. Eisenhower, 1961, Yale Law School Lillian Goldman Law Library, 1961, avalon.law.yale.edu/20th_century/eisenhower001.asp.

5. United States Office of the Under Secretary of Defense for Acquisition and Sustainment. "Report to Congress Section 889 of the FY 2018 NDAA Report on Defense Contracting Fraud." U.S. Department of Defense, December 2018, https://fas.org/man/eprint/contract-fraud.pdf

6. "These Atomic Bomb Tests Used U.S. Troops as Guinea Pigs." Smithsonian.com, Smithsonian

Institution, www.smithsonianmag.com/videos/category/history/these-atomic-bomb-tests-used-us-troops-as/.

7. Dickerson, Caitlin. "Secret World War II Chemical Experiments Tested Troops by Race." *National Public Radio*, 22 June 2015, www.npr.org/2015/06/22/415194765/u-s-troops-tested-by-race-in-secret-world-war-ii-chemical-experiments

8. https://emergency.cdc.gov/agent/sulfurmustard/basics/facts.asp

9. Hixenbaugh, Mike, and Charles Ornstein. "For Decades, the VA Turned to 1 Man on Whether Agent Orange Harmed Vets. His Reliable Answer: No." Pilotonline.com, *The Virginian-Pilot*, 26 Oct. 2016, www.pilotonline.com/military/article_f6b15a6f-acc6-5360-9a38-f6e6d31021c1.html

10. Hixenbaugh, Mike, and Charles Ornstein. "When VA Is Deciding on Agent Orange Benefits, Science Sometimes Takes Backseat to Politics and Cost." Pilotonline.com, *The Virginian-Pilot*, 15 June 2016, www.pilotonline.com/military/article_db7bacae-3e67-564c-95ad-e10c4238cba9.html

11. Hixenbaugh, Mike, and Charles Ornstein. "For Decades, the VA Turned to 1 Man on Whether Agent Orange Harmed Vets. His Reliable Answer: No." Pilotonline.com, *The Virginian-Pilot*, 26 Oct. 2016, www.pilotonline.com/military/article_f6b15a6f-acc6-5360-9a38-f6e6d31021c1.html

12. Ornstein, Charles, and Mike Hixenbaugh. "Agent Orange Curse: Vietnam Vets Can Pass Birth Defects to Their Kids, New Data Suggests." Pilotonline.com, *The*

Virginian-Pilot, 16 Dec. 2016, www.pilotonline.com/military/article_1c284628-2dbe-510d-98a2-40b639759943.html

13. Zundel, Clara G., et al. "Rates of Chronic Medical Conditions in 1991 Gulf War Veterans Compared to the General Population." MDPI, Multidisciplinary Digital Publishing Institute, 16 Mar. 2019, www.mdpi.com/1660-4601/16/6/949/htm.

14. Kime, Patricia. "VA Gets 'F' for Persian Gulf War Claims Approvals." *Military Times*, 15 Mar. 2016, www.militarytimes.com/veterans/2016/03/15/va-gets-f-for-persian-gulf-war-claims-approvals/.

15. Urbi, Jaden. "The VA's History of Setbacks and Missteps." *CNBC*, 28 May 2018, www.cnbc.com/2018/05/28/va-veterans-affairs-history-setbacks-missteps.html.

Chapter Eight

1. King, Dr. Martin Luther. "Letter from a Birmingham Jail." African Studies Center-University of Pennsylvania, 16 Apr. 1963, www.africa.upenn.edu/Articles_Gen/Letter_Birmingham.html

2. Edwards, Frank, et al. "Risk of Being Killed by Police Use of Force in the United States by Age, Race-Ethnicity, and Sex." National Academy of Sciences, 20 Aug. 2019, www.pnas.org/content/116/34/16793

3. Staff, ACLU. "The War on Marijuana in Black and White." American Civil Liberties Union, 22 Oct. 2018, www.aclu.org/issues/smart-justice/sentencing-reform/war-marijuana-black-and-white

4. "Race and the Drug War." Drug Policy Alliance, www.drugpolicy.org/issues/race-and-drug-war

5. "11 Facts About Racial Discrimination." DoSomething. org, www.dosomething.org/us/facts/11-facts-about-racial -discrimination

6. "11 Facts About Racial Discrimination." DoSomething. org, www.dosomething.org/us/facts/11-facts-about-racial -discrimination

7. "What Is Systemic Racism? [VIDEOS]." What Is Systemic Racism?, Race Forward, 4 June 2020, www.raceforward. org/videos/systemic-racism

8. Walker, Jonathan. "Health Care System a Major Factor in African Americans' Poorer Health." Physicians for a National Health Program, June 2012, pnhp.org/news/ health-care-system-a-major-factor-in-african-americans -poorer-health/

9. Walker, Jonathan. "Health Care System a Major Factor in African Americans' Poorer Health." Physicians for a National Health Program, June 2012, pnhp.org/news/health-care- system-a-major-factor-in-african-americans-poorer-health/

10. "11 Facts About Racial Discrimination." DoSomething. org, www.dosomething.org/us/facts/11-facts-about -racial-discrimination

11. "11 Facts About Racial Discrimination." DoSomething. org, www.dosomething.org/us/facts/11-facts-about -racial-discrimination

12. "11 Facts About Racial Discrimination." DoSomething. org, www.dosomething.org/us/facts/11-facts-about -racial-discrimination

13. "Racial Economic Inequality." Inequality.org, inequality. org/facts/racial-inequality/

14. "Racial Economic Inequality." Inequality.org, inequality. org/facts/racial-inequality/

15. "Racial Economic Inequality." Inequality.org, inequality. org/facts/racial-inequality/

16. Bruenig, Matt. "The Top 10 Percent of White Families Own Almost Everything." The American Prospect, Demos, 8 Sept. 2014, prospect.org/power/top-10-percent-white-families -almost-everything/

17. "23 Billion." *EdBuild*, Mar. 2019, edbuild.org/ content/23-billion

18. Lutton, Linda, et al. "Home Loans in Chicago: One Dollar to White Neighborhoods, 12 Cents to Black." *Home Mortgage Lending Inequality in Chicago*, WBEZ, 3 June 2020, inter-active.wbez.org/2020/banking/disparity/

19. "2016 Hate Crime Statistics." Federal Bureau of Investigation, 13 Nov. 2017, www.fbi.gov/news/stories/2016 -hate-crime-statistics

20. "2018 Hate Crime Statistics Released." Federal Bureau of Investigation, 12 Nov. 2019, www.fbi.gov/news/ stories/2018-hate-crime-statistics-released-111219

21. Taylor, Ryan. "Kimberly Latrice Jones BLM Video Speech Transcript." Rev, 8 June 2020, www.rev.com/blog/transcripts/ kimberly-latrice-jones-blm-video-speech-transcript

Chapter Nine

1. Millhiser, Ian. "Never Count on the Supreme Court to Protect Voting Rights." *The New Republic*, 22 Mar. 2015, newrepublic.com/article/121323/supreme-courts-history -voting-rights-injustices-excerpt

2. "Reconstruction in America: EJI Report." EJI Reports, 7 July 2020, eji.org/report/reconstruction-in-america/

3. "Voting Irregularities in Florida During the 2000 Presidential Election." Executive Summary, United States Civil Rights

Commission, June 2001, www.usccr.gov/pubs/vote2000/report/exesum.htm

4. "Missouri, 2000." Brennan Center for Justice, 10 Nov. 2007, www.brennancenter.org/our-work/research-reports/missouri-2000

5. "*Shelby County v. Holder.*" Brennan Center for Justice, 4 Aug. 2018, www.brennancenter.org/our-work/court-cases/shelby-county-v-holder

6. Caputo, Angela, et al. "How a Massive Voter Purge in Georgia Affected the 2018 Election." *APM Reports*, 29 Oct. 2019, www.apmreports.org/story/2019/10/29/georgia-voting-registration-records-removed

7. Judd, Alan. "Georgia's Strict Laws Lead to Large Purge of Voters." *The Atlanta Journal-Constitution*, 30 Oct. 2018, www.ajc.com/news/state--regional-govt--politics/voter-purge-begs-question-what-the-matter-with-georgia/YAFvuk3Bu95kJIMaDiDFqJ/

8. Rouan, Rick. "Vast Majority of the 180,000 Ohio Voters Purged Because They Didn't Vote." *The Columbus Dispatch*, 39 Sept. 2019, www.dispatch.com/news/20190930/vast-majority-of-180000-ohio-voters-purged-because-they-didnt-vote

9. Caputo, Angela, et al. "How a Massive Voter Purge in Georgia Affected the 2018 Election." *APM Reports*

10. Ingraham, Christopher. "Analysis: This Anti-Voter-Fraud Program Gets It Wrong Over 99 Percent of the Time. The GOP Wants to Take It Nationwide." *The Washington Post*, WP Company, 20 July 2017, www.washingtonpost.com/news/wonk/wp/2017/07/20/this-anti-voter-fraud-program-gets-it-wrong-over-99-of-the-time-the-gop-wants-to-take-it-nationwide/

11. Levitt, Justin. "A Comprehensive Investigation of Voter Impersonation Finds 31 Credible Incidents out of One

Billion Ballots Cast." *The Washington Post*, WP Company, 6 Aug. 2014, www.washingtonpost.com/news/wonk/wp/2014/08/06/a-comprehensive-investigation-of-voter-impersonation-finds-31-credible-incidents-out-of-one-billion-ballots-cast/

12. "Voter ID." Georgia Department of Driver Services, dds.georgia.gov/voter-id

13. Horwitz, Sari. "Getting a Photo ID so You Can Vote Is Easy. Unless You're Poor, Black, Latino or Elderly." *The Washington Post*, WP Company, 23 May 2016, www.washingtonpost.com/politics/courts_law/getting-a-photo-id-so-you-can-vote-is-easy-unless-youre-poor-black-latino-or-elderly/2016/05/23/8d5474ec-20f0-11e6-8690-f14ca9de2972_story.html

14. Anderson, Carol. *One Person, No Vote: How Voter Suppression Is Destroying Our Democracy*. Bloomsbury Publishing, 2019. 60-61

15. Anderson, *One Person, No Vote*, 57

16. "Public Housing ID Not Valid Voter Photo ID in Alabama." NAACP Legal Defense and Educational Fund, 4 Nov. 2014, www.naacpldf.org/press-release/public-housing-id-not-valid-voter-photo-id-in-alabama/

17. Reilly, Ryan J. "Judges Seem Ready to Mess With Texas' Voter ID Law." Talking Points Memo, 13 July 2012, talkingpointsmemo.com/muckraker/judges-seem-ready-to-mess-with-texas-voter-id-law

18. Johnson, Theodore R., and Max Feldman. "The New Voter Suppression." Brennan Center for Justice, 16 Jan. 2020, www.brennancenter.org/our-work/research-reports/new-voter-suppression

19. Maxwell, Connor, and Danielle Root. "Five Truths About Voter Suppression." Center for American Progress,

12 Mar. 2017, www.americanprogress.org/issues/race/news/2017/05/12/432339/five-truths-voter-suppression/

20. Horwitz, Sari. "Getting a Photo ID so You Can Vote Is Easy. Unless You're Poor, Black, Latino or Elderly." *The Washington Post*, WP Company, 23 May 2016, www.washingtonpost.com/politics/courts_law/getting-a-photo-id-so-you-can-vote-is-easy-unless-youre-poor-black-latino-or-elderly/2016/05/23/8d5474ec-20f0-11e6-8690-f14ca9de2972_story.html

21. *Voter Registration Statistics*, North Carolina State Board of Elections, 27 June 2020, vt.ncsbe.gov/RegStat/Results/?date=06%2F27%2F2020

22. Daley, David. "The Secret Files of the Master of Modern Republican Gerrymandering." *The New Yorker*, 6 Sept. 2019, www.newyorker.com/news/news-desk/the-secret-files-of-the-master-of-modern-republican-gerrymandering

23. Daley, David. "The Secret Files of the Master of Modern Republican Gerrymandering."

24. "Democrats Cry Foul as House Republicans Redraw District Lines." *The Atlanta Journal-Constitution*, 9 Mar. 2017, www.ajc.com/news/state--regional-govt--politics/democrats-cry-foul-house-republicans-redraw-district-lines/sOOXVi3vMCWJCB7gpAntTN/

25. Berman, Ari. "Texas's Redistricting Maps and Voter-ID Law Intentionally Discriminated Against Minority Voters." *The Nation*, 13 Mar. 2017, www.thenation.com/article/archive/texass-redistricting-maps-and-voter-id-law-intentionally-discriminated-against-minority-voters/

26. Wolf, Thomas. "Bringing Whitford Into Focus. What You Should Know About One of the Most Pivotal Cases in Decades on How Congressional Maps Are Drawn., Brennan

Center for Justice, 8 Aug. 2017, www.brennancenter.org/
our-work/analysis-opinion/bringing-whitford-focus.

27. Daley, David. "Meet the Man Who May End
     Gerrymandering: A Retired Wisconsin Law Professor's
     Supreme Court Case Could Save Democracy." Salon.com,
     26 Mar. 2017, www.salon.com/2017/03/26/meet-the-man-
     who-may-end-gerrymandering-a-retired-wisconsin-law-
     professors-supreme-court-case-could-save-democracy/

28. Lau, Tim. *Citizens United Explained.* Brennan Center for
     Justice, 12 Dec. 2019, www.brennancenter.org/our-work/
     research-reports/citizens-united-explained

Chapter Ten

1.   Sargrad, Scott, et al. "A Quality Education for Every
     Child." Center for American Progress, 2 June 2019,
     www.americanprogress.org/issues/education-k-12/
     reports/2019/07/02/471511/quality-education
     -every-child/

2.   Jacob, Brian A. "How the U.S. Department of Education
     Can Foster Education Reform in the Era of Trump and
     ESSA." The Brookings Institution, 2 Feb. 2017, www.brook-
     ings.edu/research/how-the-u-s-department-of-education-
     can-foster-education-reform-in-the-era-of-trump-and-essa/

3.   "K-12 Facts." The Center for Education Reform, 19 Dec.
     2019, edreform.com/2012/04/k-12-facts/#Snapshot

4.   DeSilver, Drew. "U.S. Academic Achievement Lags That
     of Many Other Countries." Pew Research Center, 15 Feb.
     2017, www.pewresearch.org/fact-tank/2017/02/15/u-s-stu-
     dents-internationally-math-science/

5.   "The NCES Fast Facts Tool Provides Quick Answers
     to Many Education Questions." National Center for

Education Statistics (NCES) Home Page, a Part of the U.S. Department of Education, 2016, nces.ed.gov/fastfacts /display.asp?id=1

6. "The State of America's Children 2020—Child Poverty." Children's Defense Fund, 18 Feb. 2020, www.childrens-defense.org/policy/resources/soac-2020-child-poverty/

7. McGuire, Kent. "Time to Put Poverty Back on the Education Reform Agenda." *Philanthropy News Digest*, Candid, 19 May 2014, philanthropynewsdigest.org/commentary-and-opinion/ time-to-put-poverty-back-on-the-education-reform-agenda.

8. "K-12 Disparity Facts and Statistics." United Negro College Fund, uncf.org/pages/k-12-disparity-facts-and-stats.

9. Jackson, C. K., Johnson, R. C., & Persico, C. (2016). The effects of school spending on educational and economic outcomes: Evidence from school finance reforms. *Quarterly Journal of Economics*, 131(1), 157-218. [qjv036]. https://doi. org/10.1093/qje/qjv036

10. Sargrad, Scott, et al. "A Quality Education for Every Child."

11. Garcia, Emma, and Elaine Weiss. "U.S. Schools Struggle to Hire and Retain Teachers: The Second Report in 'The Perfect Storm in the Teacher Labor Market' Series." Economic Policy Institute, 16 Apr. 2019, www.epi.org/publication/u-s-schools-struggle-to-hire-and-retain-teachers-the-second-re-port-in-the-perfect-storm-in-the-teacher-labor-market-series/

12. Carver-Thomas, Desiree, and Linda Darling-Hammond. "Teacher Turnover: Why It Matters and What We Can Do About It." Learning Policy Institute, Aug. 2017, learning-policyinstitute.org/sites/default/files/product-files/Teacher_ Turnover_REPORT.pdf

13. Garcia, Emma, and Elaine Weiss. "U.S. Schools Struggle to Hire and Retain Teachers: The Second Report in 'The Perfect

Storm in the Teacher Labor Market' Series." Economic Policy Institute, 16 Apr. 2019, www.epi.org/publication/u-s-schools-struggle-to-hire-and-retain-teachers-the-second-report-in-the-perfect-storm-in-the-teacher-labor-market-series/

14. "Our Mission." *YouCubed*, www.youcubed.org/our-mission/

15. Spector, Carrie. "Schools That Received State Funds to Expand Career Training Programs Saw Lower Dropout Rates, Stanford Researcher Finds." Stanford Graduate School of Education, 15 May 2019, ed.stanford.edu/news/schools-received-state-funds-expand-career-training-programs-saw-lower-dropout-rates-stanford#:~:text=A%20new%20study%20by%20a,a%20doctoral%20candidate%20at%20Stanford

Chapter Eleven

1. Stolberg, Sheryl Gay. "The Art of Political Distraction." *The New York Times*, 21 Mar. 2009, www.nytimes.com/2009/03/22/weekinreview/22stolberg.html?mtrref=www.google.com&gwh=F900AD35B3B-4CE3210542D852DB3D015&gwt=%E2%80%A6

2. Tierney, Dominic. "The Risks of Foreign Policy as Political Distraction." *The Atlantic*, Atlantic Media Company, 15 June 2017, www.theatlantic.com/international/archive/2017/06/trump-diversionary-foreign-policy/530079/

3. Leibovich, Mark. "The Politics of Distraction." *The New York Times*, 1 Sept. 2015, www.nytimes.com/2015/09/06/magazine/the-politics-of-distraction.html?auth=linked-google

Chapter Twelve

1. Heath, Dan. *Upstream: The Quest to Solve Problems Before They Happen*. Avid Reader Press, 2020.

2. "The Thomas Jefferson Hour." *National Public Radio.* February 5, 2019. Radio

Chapter Thirteen

1. Reinhart, RJ. "Majority in U.S. Still Say a Third Party Is Needed." *Gallup.com*, Gallup, 26 Oct. 2018, news.gallup. com/poll/244094/majority-say-third-party-needed.aspx.

ABOUT THE AUTHOR

David Brandt has nearly three decades of experience in communications, first as a journalist and then as a public affairs professional. He holds a Master of Arts degree in journalism from Regent University and a Bachelor of Arts degree in political science from Westminster College. He and his wife make their home in North Carolina and have two grown children.

I hope you enjoyed this book.
If so, would you do me a favor?

Like all authors, I rely on online reviews to encourage future sales. Your opinion is invaluable. Would you take a few moments now to share your assessment of my book on Amazon or any other book-review website you prefer? Your opinion will help the book marketplace become more transparent and useful to all.

Thank you very much!

Made in the USA
Las Vegas, NV
20 January 2021